DEDICATION

To my wife, Staci, and my daughters, Ally and Delaney, who have been so gracious and patient, allowing me to steal the necessary time away to complete this project

Mark A. Nash

To my family, who always understands the hard work and dedication it takes to bring a book to press

Sheila R. Poling

TABLE OF CONTENTS

CONTENTS

ACKNOWLEDGMENTS

The authors would like to thank all the organizations and individuals who have shared their stories and experiences with us and to acknowledge all of their hard work as we observed and challenged them in seeking a balanced approach to both Lean and Six Sigma.

We would also like to acknowledge the Oklahoma Alliance for Manufacturing Excellence, Grand Lake Manufacturers Council, Oklahoma Department of Career and Technology Education, and all of the Black Belt, Green Belt, and Lean class participants we have taught and coached. Without these dedicated individuals, we would not have the remarkable case studies presented in this work.

We would be remiss, however, if we did not single out the members of the first Six Sigma Black Belt class from Metzeler Automotive Profile Systems, a group of dedicated lean practitioners who saw that there had to be a way to move their organization to the next level. This group gave us the idea of a synchronized approach to using Lean and Six Sigma in which the initiatives could not only coexist but excel within a continuous improvement environment.

A heartfelt word of thanks to Billie Miller, executive assistant, Pinnacle Partners, Inc., for her work on this book, and to the editors and staff at Productivity Press. The authors are especially indebted to Michael Sinnochi, senior acquisitions editor of Productivity Press, without whose interest and support this book would not have been written.

INTRODUCTION

Lean or Six Sigma?

Lean? Six Sigma? Lean Six Sigma? Lean and Six Sigma have both become increasingly popular as continuous improvement initiatives over the past several years, and many organizations are struggling with a dilemma that these two approaches have spawned: whether to go down the Lean path, or the Six Sigma path, or merge the approaches into a single effort called Lean Six Sigma. This basic question about approach was one of the core issues that the authors confronted when deciding to write this book. Realizing that most Lean and Six Sigma practitioners in the field were also struggling with this question of approach, we began the work by exploring their answers.

The most common answer to these questions among Lean practitioners was, "Use Lean until you run out of Lean opportunities." Six Sigma Black Belts usually responded by saying "Use Six Sigma. After all, it is statistically based and provides actual data to back up the changes required to reduce variation and improve quality within your processes." More recently, some Lean and Six Sigma practitioners are advocating an approach that combines the quantitative power of Six Sigma with the speed of Lean. So what is the right answer? Or more importantly, are any of these three answers correct?

Comparing our own experiences with Lean and Six Sigma, we began to discover patterns and ideas that provided many intriguing insights into this broad question. What we found was compelling enough to drive us toward sharing our knowledge and experiences with others. Along the way, in the process of fine-tuning basic theories and ideas, some of our initial opinions have changed multiple times. What has remained an unwavering constant is the underlying premise that Lean and Six Sigma should be used in a synchronized approach. This approach (which is discussed in detail in Chapter 8) allows for faster results in Six Sigma projects and stronger more powerful Lean results through the quick-hitting use of Six Sigma tools when appropriate. Perhaps the most significant theme that emerged during our exploration of the subject is that this synchronized approach provides optimal results when performed in a sequential manner: using lean thinking and methodology to eliminate "low-hanging fruit" (i.e., obvious waste) and then attacking variation and defect problems through Six Sigma projects.

What we have come to recognize is that this synchronized methodology does not try to complete Six Sigma projects in 30 days or turn Lean teams into statisticians. The underlying goal is to assist the process improvement team to do the following:

- To use the right tools at the right time
- To maximize results
- To complete projects as quickly as possible within the constraints of the methodologies

Obviously, no single book can provide all of the answers to an important question, and this book is no exception. It is a step that will, no doubt, be part of a long exploratory path that we (and others) will continue to travel, often making dramatic forays into new territory. Jack Welch has stated the need for setting big goals and forcing employees into sometimes drastic or dramatic action. During the IQPC Lean Six Sigma Summit West in October of 2005, Welch explained his dramatic demand for process improvement as a way to get results: "Going over to the extreme side to move the needle is what you must do to get people motivated."

As Six Sigma professionals continue to look for ways to change the culture and motivate the workforce into making process change a reality, the idea of Lean's fast-paced approach to process improvement has become one way of quickly starting the process of moving the needle over to this "extreme" side. Doing things differently has a major impact on a process and gets the workforce involved. Is a synchronized methodology the right approach? We don't have all the answers, but what we have seen and experienced to date supports this concept and is a springboard for additional study.

Every day we ask ourselves new questions about how Lean and Six Sigma blend together to create a truly synchronized and fully integrated approach to continuous improvement. This book's purpose is to provide some answers to the basic questions concerning this blend and to serve as a guide to understanding the power of both methodologies. Our intent is to show how Lean and Six Sigma can work together and to challenge you to think about (or rethink) the strategy your organization currently uses.

If you have not yet adopted either approach and are looking for the "right" toolset for continuous improvement, this book should prove useful in sorting out the various statements and stances that exist in today's strategy-focused world of continuous improvement. If we have succeeded, the ideas presented in this book will inspire you to find answers by asking new questions each and every day and searching for the perfect blend of tools and techniques to achieve your organization's strategic goals and objectives.

How this Book Is Organized

This book is not full of flowery proverbs and feel-good stories. It contains down-to-earth practical explanations and techniques used to give organizations the competitive advantage they must achieve to survive and thrive in the marketplace.

Chapters 1 through 3 provide the framework for the book: Chapter 1 reviews the purpose and goals of implementing either Lean or Six Sigma; chapter 2 offers a thorough review of the benefits of using Lean; and chapter 3 provides a similar discussion of the benefits of Six Sigma.

Chapter 4 illustrates the *differences* between the two approaches and discusses the limitations of using only one approach or the other. Chapter 5 describes the challenges of making the change to a Lean environment and the different challenges of making the change to a Six Sigma environment.

Chapters 6 through 9 address the benefits of applying *both* Lean and Six Sigma to an organization. Chapter 6 examines how Six Sigma results can be applied to a Lean culture. Chapter 7 offers guidelines for choosing which methodology will work best for different projects. Chapter 8 shows how to *synchronize* the two approaches. Finally, chapter 9 serves as a wrap-up that encourages looking beyond individual projects and focusing on long-term continuous improvement.

Interspersed throughout the book are eight detailed case studies that illustrate the use of Lean, Six Sigma, or a combined or synchronized approach. Each includes a discussion of the problem the organizations implementing these respective strategies faced, the reasons they adopted particular solutions, and the results achieved. In addition, chapter 6 features a detailed study of almost sixty projects in both manufacturing and health-care organizations that used Lean, Six Sigma, or some combination of both—and the results achieved in those projects.

THE PURPOSE OF
a LEAN OR SIX
SIGMA INITIATIVE

"Every morning in Africa, a gazelle awakens.
He has only one thought on his mind:
To be able to run faster than the fastest lion.
If he cannot, then he will be eaten.

Every morning in Africa, a lion awakens.
He has only one thought on his mind:
To be able to run faster than the slowest gazelle.
If he cannot, he will die of hunger.

Whether you choose to be a gazelle or a lion is
    of no consequence.
It is enough to know that with the rising of the
    sun, you must run.
And you must run faster than you did yesterday
    or you will die.

This is the race of life."

AFRICAN PROVERB

What is the real purpose of a Lean initiative? A Six Sigma initiative?
Is it to run and manage process improvement projects systematically?
Is it to become a Lean or Six Sigma "world-class" organization? Or

is it to eliminate waste or reduce variation in our processes? And if we ask these questions, shouldn't we also ask, "Why are we in business? What is the ultimate goal of our organization?"

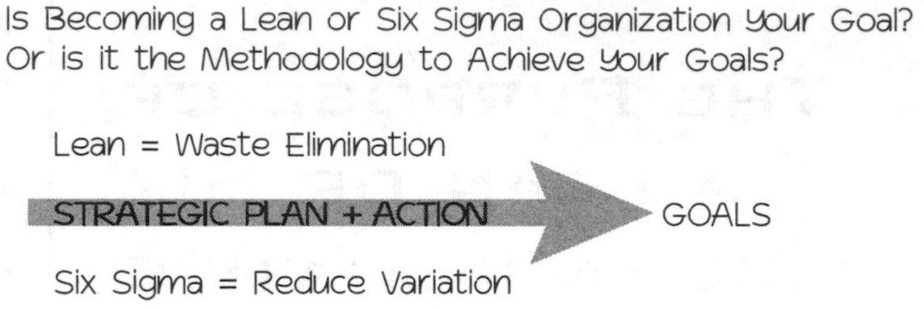

Is Becoming a Lean or Six Sigma Organization Your Goal? Or is it the Methodology to Achieve Your Goals?

Lean = Waste Elimination

STRATEGIC PLAN + ACTION ➤ GOALS

Six Sigma = Reduce Variation

Figure 1-1.

As Figure 1-1 illustrates, these two very powerful continuous improvement initiatives can help you accomplish several things. They can

- assist your organization to meet your strategic goals by improving your processes;
- grow the top line;
- improve the bottom line;
- increase quality and customer satisfaction.

Lean and Six Sigma work individually and as part of a coordinated initiative, taking advantage of the power of both disciplines. The ultimate result of either or both approaches is the creation of a competitive advantage based on successful implementation.

In a typical organization, data are collected, analyzed, and reported, quite often without any real relevance to the issues and opportunities of the organization. This is an example of Albert Einstein's "not everything that can be counted, counts" concept. Using a cookie-cutter approach or a "this is how I was trained" approach often leads to false gains, untrue "reported savings," or work for the sake of work. It does not even begin to reflect the reason to utilize Lean and/or Six Sigma. Indeed, knowing the reason lies at the heart of the matter.

Einstein's quote about counting is especially apropos when you consider what some organizations do when starting up their Lean and/or Six Sigma efforts. Many organizations go down the Lean, Six

Sigma, or even the Lean Six Sigma path without answers to some very basic questions. They start process improvement without a clear vision of their ultimate goal. They measure things that may or may not have any value to the strategic goals and mission of their companies. When things do not improve, they blame the approach or methodology without considering the way it was envisioned or implemented.

Gain Competitive Advantage

In today's global economy, you can never overstate the value of gaining a competitive advantage. As an organization looks to retain and gain market share or provide products or services that its customers truly want, the ultimate goal should be continuous improvement. If an organization, regardless of size, ever stops looking for a better way to do business or stops looking for better quality and lower prices, the competition will gain momentum and take that organization's market share. Eventually, the stagnant organization will die (see Fig. 1-2).

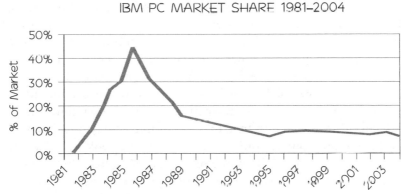

Many Lean practitioners look to the rise and fall of IBM in the personal computer industry as the motivation to dedicate uncompromising effort to Lean. IBM changed the world with their introduction of the PC in the early 1980s, quickly taking more than 40 percent of the market share. However, IBM was unable to maintain this market share as customer demands and expectations changed rapidly throughout the 80s and 90s. IBM eventually exited the PC industry in 2004 by selling its PC Division to Lenovo after suffering significant losses from 2000 to 2004.

Figure 1-2.

To survive, a business must stay ahead of the competition. Gaining this competitive advantage is becoming more and more difficult. Moreover, as Lean and Six Sigma continue to grow in popularity and the success stories multiply, the sheer number of organizations choosing these approaches to tackle process improvement will make it more difficult to acquire the desired edge. However, if the disciplines and methodologies of Lean and/or Six Sigma are adhered to, and if your organization truly approaches these methodologies as a continuous improvement initiative to meet your strategic goals, you will find that advantage. The reason is simple: The real use of continuous improvement forces you to stay ahead of your competition by continually reevaluating and improving your position in the marketplace because "good enough" today is never "good enough" for tomorrow.

A related question is whether the efforts are focused on continual growth or incremental growth. Too many managers at the top of organizations look for incremental improvements made by starting a new strategic initiative, pronounce huge savings and improvements, and then move on to the next buzz word in management theory. By approaching process improvement in this manner, an organization changes an initiative into a "program." Unfortunately, all programs, by their very nature, start and stop. Over time, the workforce becomes numb to this flavor-of-the-month approach to business. Figure 1-3 illustrates the difference between an incremental, flavor-of-the-month approach and a continued growth approach.

Lean and Six Sigma, used as they were originally intended, launch an integrated, strategy-focused, continuous improvement initiative that never ends. In adopting this initiative, you will always be listening to your customers' expectations and looking for a way to process "perfection." This one big goal must remain on the forefront throughout the strategic planning process. It is, essentially, a commitment to excellence. Some Six Sigma practitioners call this "Organization and Operations Excellence." For many Lean practitioners, it is the "Pursuit of Perfection." And although your organization may never fully reach this goal of perfect excellence, the journey—with your customers' expectations guiding you—will inevitably result in improvement and will frequently lead to the results you are seeking. Figure 1.4 illustrates how customer expectations drive this process.

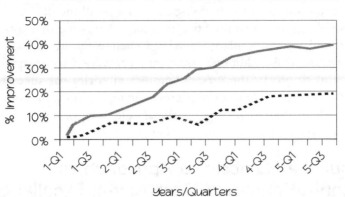

COMPARISON OF IMPROVEMENT STRATEGIES

··· Incremental Improvement   — Continuous Improvement

The chart above demonstrates the slow progression toward savings using the incremental, or flavor-of-the-month, approach to process improvement. Since employees are not able to see "real" change, they can become numb to the need for change. The continuous improvement approach allows you to achieve dramatic improvements that continue to grow.

Figure 1-3.

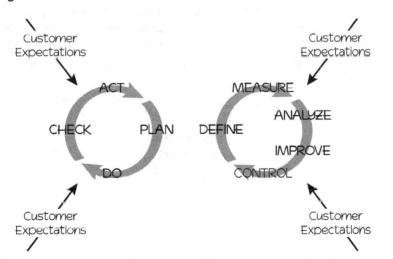

The basic concept of continuous improvement is put into action through the methodology utilized by each discipline; "Plan, Do, Check, Act" or PDCA for Lean and "DMAIC" for Six Sigma. Because more organizations are beginning to intertwine their efforts, there is a move to use DMAIC as the underlying methodology for Lean project management.

Figure 1-4.

Understanding that the Lean and Six Sigma initiatives are continuous improvement methodologies can make all the difference in successfully gaining a competitive advantage. Knowing that you can and should return regularly to where change (good or bad) has occurred and make additional improvements will set you apart from the competition. In the process, project victories (or successes), regardless of size, will not only improve the top and bottom lines but will also help change the organizational culture to bring the workforce on board with Lean and Six Sigma.

Acquire a Structured Approach to Organizational and Operational Excellence

To achieve a competitive advantage by using Lean and Six Sigma, your organization must develop a structured approach to organizational and operational excellence. Without this structure, an organization is doomed to repeat the failures of so many other companies that attack process improvement without understanding the impact on the entire organization. Top management must lead the effort. There must be a structured process in place to manage top-down commitment, and there must be organization-wide, bottom-up implementation. The strategic goals of the organization must be the focus of both of these integrated initiatives from day one (see Fig. 1-5).

6

Management
Commitment

STRATEGIC GOALS

Employee Involved
Implementation

Figure 1-5.

Long term, there is little benefit from starting down the continuous improvement path if you are not improving what is important to the success of your organization. To define what is important to your organization, you must understand and capture what is important to your customers—the "voice of the customer" (see Fig. 1-6). If the voice of the customer is ignored, all the effort to improve your processes and ultimately your top and bottom lines will be a waste. If you are spending time, effort, and money on things your customers are not willing to pay for, you are creating more waste!

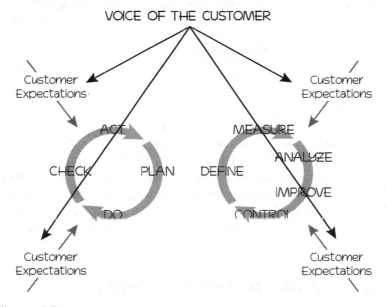

Figure 1-6.

Because the methodologies of Lean and Six Sigma blend into an integrated initiative, Lean and Six Sigma efforts can and should be implemented and managed simultaneously. Although the two disciplines have very similar goals, however, they approach improvement from different directions (see Fig. 1-7), and one of the overarching purposes of this work is to show how and why *implementing Lean first* provides faster Six Sigma results when both initiatives are done properly.

As the figure illustrates, the two methodologies have two distinct targets. But implemented and managed in a coordinated manner,

7

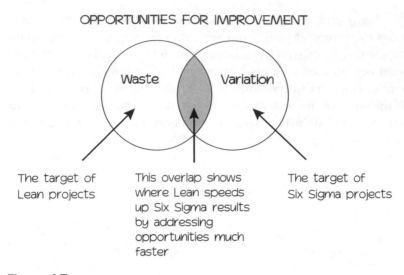

Figure 1-7.

they should overlap to create a single strategic focus. Is this a unique concept or just common sense? It may be both. Based on other philosophies and strategies to using Lean and Six Sigma together, this approach seems unique. Stepping back and looking at the foundational goals and underlying principles of both continuous improvement initiatives, you will see the common sense behind this integrated structure.

Focus on Strategy-driven Results

If an organization's goals are to grow the top line, improve the bottom line, and improve customer satisfaction through process improvement, using multiple approaches simultaneously must be a *coordinated effort*. But the coordination should be through *strategic implementation*, not *consolidated management*. The approaches are different. The methods, on the surface, are different. The speed and pace and purpose of implementation are very different.

Many continuous improvement practitioners attempt to create a single effort by combining strategies or methodologies, usually as a way to save time and money. The premise behind this is that the more methodologies, tools, and techniques that we can combine, the less time it will take, thereby lowering all costs and speeding up results. By combining two efforts into one, however, many companies find that one of the two initiatives gets "watered down" while the other becomes more dominant. The result is having to choose which of the efforts will be compromised and what will be cut?

Which effort will be compromised? Dr. W. Edwards Deming used to refer to the concept of cutting necessary steps when implementing a strategic methodology as companies looking for "instant pudding." This approach seldom produces the desired results, often because focus is ambiguous or misdirected. The focus of combined management should be at the *executive and strategic level*, identifying where and on what to focus your Lean and Six Sigma continuous improvement efforts. Then, by allowing Lean to operate at its optimal pace, without excessive restraints by management, the organization can take advantage of the momentum and create employee involvement.

By creating common understanding of the need for change, and by allowing employees to participate in Lean projects where results are seen in weeks as opposed to months or years, a strong foundation for change is established, along with a culture that enables change (see Fig. 1-8). Thus, when Six Sigma projects are launched, the workforce more readily accepts them. If they are prepared for change, workers

Category	Lean	Six Sigma	Lean & Six Sigma
Selective Employee Training		X	X
All Employee Training	X		X
Common Understanding of the Need to Change	X		X
Project Participation by Selected Employees		X	X
Project Participation by All Employees	X		X
Project Participation by Management	X	X (limited*)	X

*Management participation in Six Sigma projects is often limited to the role of Champion, Executive Council member, or periodic project updates and/or reviews

Figure 1-8. Cultural Impact of Lean and/or Six Sigma

are willing to provide input and assist with implementation because they know that change is real and can make the work tasks more efficient and effective.

How and when you select a Lean or Six Sigma project path is where the differentiation occurs. Consider, for example, the difference in the underlying thrust of these methodologies:

- Lean focuses on identifying and eliminating waste.
- Six Sigma focuses on reducing variability and eliminating defects in the process.

Then consider the implications of implementation and the impact of one on the other. Lean projects are quite often inexpensive, fast-paced events, attacking low-hanging fruit. The end results, financially, of this type of project may swing wildly from week to week, event to event. The financial goals and long-term quality issues and objectives of a particular project target may not meet the minimum criteria established for a Six Sigma project, or they may cause it to be ranked much lower on the Six Sigma potential project list. These types of opportunities are perfect Lean targets. Long term, the low-hanging fruit is removed, processes are quite often more predictable and streamlined. Then the effort applied through Six Sigma produces results much faster because you can focus on fewer but more meaningful opportunities (see Fig. 1-9).

Understanding the role and direction of both Lean and Six Sigma allows an organization to focus on strategic results. Utilizing a results-driven approach provides the focal point for staying the course and trying to attain perfection. Without this focus, an organization will drift, often in one or both of the following ways:

- Project creep will appear as each manager starts looking for his or her own vision of success.
- The overall intent and purpose of the process improvement effort will change as management changes.

But with a results-driven approach, management can look directly at the most recent results, compare them with long-term results, and stay focused on the strategic goals—the very reason for embarking on this journey.

Continually reminding the entire organization of the continuous improvement path and the objectives, keeps everyone through-

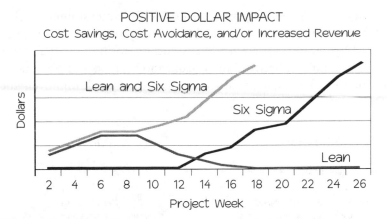

POSITIVE DOLLAR IMPACT
Cost Savings, Cost Avoidance, and/or Increased Revenue

The basic trend lines for average impact reports from a sampling of projects conducted from 2001 to 2005 shows the expected trends for projects where only Lean was used, where only Six Sigma was used, and where the two disciplines were integrated. Whereas Six Sigma projects typically did not start showing dollar impact until the third or fourth month, Lean projects began to show smaller weekly returns after as little as eight weeks of project work in an area. By integrating the two approaches, it is possible to start Six Sigma projects faster and show results sooner since the focus of many projects is more refined.

Figure 1-9.   11

out the company working toward the same goals. Lean and Six Sigma work as an integrated yet coordinated effort, where Lean opportunities are *continuously* pursued and Six Sigma projects are defined and pursued on an *as-needed* basis. Lean teams will continue to function during Six Sigma projects and be available to act when Lean opportunities arise. In contrast, Six Sigma teams will be eliminated or disbanded at the end of each project because they pass the newly improved process back to the process owners.

Throughout the strategic implementation process, it is critical to remember two inseparable components that have an impact on your business. The first of these concerns the organization and the second concerns customer expectations. With these two components in mind, you ultimately must produce top-line growth. Businesses have a right to produce products and offer services that yield the highest possible profits. Similarly, customers have the right to expect to purchase the highest quality products and receive the highest quality services at the lowest possible cost. This fundamental acknowledgement of business's *and* customers' rights and expectations is known as the "value proposition" (see Fig. 1-10). Organizations must use this value proposition to establish a strategic alignment between the organization's rights and customers' expectations. This strategic alignment is critical to all improvement efforts.

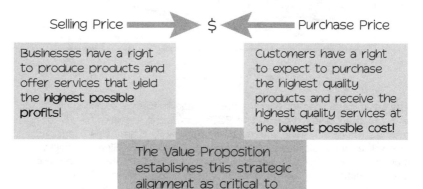

Selling Price ➡ $ ⬅ Purchase Price

Businesses have a right to produce products and offer services that yield the **highest possible profits!**

Customers have a right to expect to purchase the highest quality products and receive the highest quality services at the **lowest possible cost!**

The Value Proposition establishes this strategic alignment as critical to all improvement efforts

12   **Figure 1-10.**

Improve Top-line Growth

Lean and Six Sigma help the organization with top-line growth. Lean will very rapidly assist by

- standardizing basic flow concepts;
- eliminating non–value-added steps and tasks in the process;
- ultimately creating more capacity and throughput.

Jim Womack, author of *Lean Thinking*, stated that Lean thinking specifically helps managers clearly specify value (by specific product) by

- lining up all the value-creating activities for a specific product along a value stream;
- making value flow smoothly without interruption, thereby letting the customer pull value from the producer, while allowing the producer to pursue perfection.

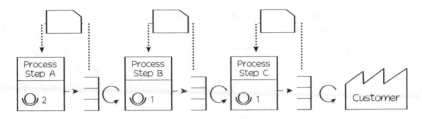

Figure 1-11. Creating Flow Through Pull Systems

Six Sigma can and will help organizations reduce process variations and decrease defects as the processes run faster. When you control these issues through a structured approach, positive results come much more quickly. Without a controlled initiative to top-line growth, your costs will most certainly grow as well.

Achieve Better Bottom-line Results

An obvious outcome of increased capacity and throughput (without increased costs) is better bottom-line results. Once again, Lean and Six Sigma combine to give the organization positive results through a controlled and coordinated effort. Although Lean reduces inventory and increases throughput, Lean implementation will only take you so far. At some point in time, the organization must look at correcting the more complex issues that Lean does not address. Six Sigma provides statistical and analytical tools needed to dissect these complex issues.

An Action Plan

1. To achieve success, you must continually focus on process improvement. As one process shows significant progress, Lean thinking says move on to the next opportunity. But, whether a project is being run as a Lean effort or a Six Sigma effort, you must remember to monitor and revisit this process. Look for new opportunities within the process when it is reviewed.
2. Additionally, you need to think about the overall integrated Lean and Six Sigma initiative. Periodically revisit this process to see if adjustments in strategy are required and to see if priorities have changed.

13

3. As your organization implements change in a process, utilize the knowledge and skills of the workforce to make change happen: This is one of the greatest keys to success and process improvement. As Womack observed, "Three attributes—taking the long view, technical virtuosity, and a passionate will to succeed—are essential for any organization making the Lean transition." If the workforce is not involved in and does not buy into the change, the possibility of failure is much higher. If the employees buy into the change, there is a natural tendency to make it work. Successful Lean and Six Sigma teams understand and use this concept to their advantage.

Conclusion

Whether you utilize Lean techniques or Six Sigma to improve a process, the goal is to improve the things that are important to your "value proposition." To succeed, project teams should focus on how to align "the voice of the process" with "the voice of the customer" (see Fig. 1-12). The voice of the process is defined as how the process is currently operating.

In the Six Sigma world, this is viewed though the use of *process behavior charts* (or *control charts*)—visual representations of the process with all its flaws and exceptions. Lean projects use *current-state maps* to obtain a similar visual picture of the voice of the process. The voice of the customer is defined as the ultimate customers' expectations in relation to quality, cost and delivery. Six Sigma uses *critical-to-quality characteristics* (CTQs) to define, measure, and set goals defined by the voice of the customer. Lean uses *future-state maps* for the same purpose. It doesn't matter which methodology you use at any given moment, as long as you are striving to satisfy the "value proposition."

Remember that *customer satisfaction* is the single measurement that predicts long-term success with process improvement. The voice of the customer should be driving all that you do; whether it is Lean or Six Sigma. When your customers see process improvement results that benefit them and address their concerns, then you have succeeded. If your customers see no value in the changes you made, you may not have gone far enough or you have not focused on the right opportunities. Understanding what your customers

Aligning the Voice of the Process within the **Voice of the Customer** is the goal to satisfying the **Value Proposition.**

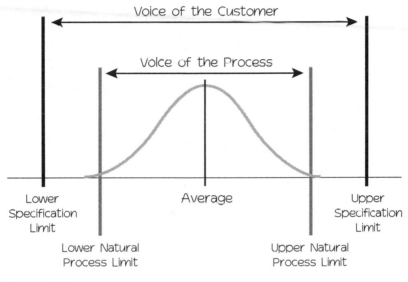

Figure 1-12.

want and expect is only half the equation—you must also deliver improvements that customers see as beneficial to them. After all, if your customers are happy, they will return and buy more!

Although your customers won't care whether you have implemented Lean or Six Sigma, it is important for you to have a clear understanding of both approaches before attempting integration. In connection with this, the next two chapters examine each methodology separately. Chapter 2 describes Lean in detail, and chapter 3 describes Six Sigma in detail.

> *Getting up every morning, running and staying*
> *ahead of the competition, this is the answer.*
> *It doesn't matter if you are a lion or a gazelle.*

The Power and Focus of Lean

Lean is a systematic approach to identifying
and eliminating waste through continuous
improvement by flowing the product or service
at the pull of your customer in
pursuit of perfection.

—The NIST/Manufacturing Extension Partnership
Lean Network definition of Lean

Lean is a powerful continuous improvement initiative that is highly focused and employee dependent. The simplicity of the Lean tools, combined with a systematic implementation methodology, allows all employees of the organization to participate in process improvement. Yet the most powerful aspect of Lean is not what participants do to *add to* or *improve* a process but what they *remove* from the process to improve it.

Eliminate Waste in All Processes

The primary focus of Lean is often stated as *identifying and eliminating waste from the product or service provided* (see Fig. 2-1). Eliminating non-value-added activity sets the stage for dramatic quality improvements and customer satisfaction.

VALUE-ADDED ACTIVITY AS A PERCENTAGE
OF TOTAL PROCESS LEAD TIME

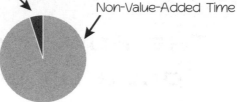

Organizations adopting Lean as a continuous improvement methodology typically find 95% of all process lead time is non-value-added.

Source: NIST/Manufacturing Extention Partnership

Figure 2-1.

This chapter reviews the Eight Wastes of Lean and provides a systematic approach to identifying and categorizing waste. Using this approach helps you determine the root cause of a problem and then take appropriate corrective action. Finding and addressing the root cause of a problem is an essential step in this process. Many people mistakenly think that removing or eliminating the waste observed is enough to resolve any related issue or problem. Over time, however, the issue or problem will resurface. In many cases, increased through-put exacerbates an original problem or issue and makes it worse.

The best way to avoid a false sense of security and prevent old problems from resurfacing in new and magnified forms is to challenge all employees on a Lean project to look for a *root cause* instead of focusing on and treating *symptoms*. Early in the Lean project cycle, this can be accomplished through issue/solution team meetings. During these meetings, team members

- identify waste, or non–value–added activities;
- classify each waste into one of the eight waste categories;
- explore the waste for root cause, identifying as many potential solutions as possible (see Fig. 2-2).

As Lean improvements are made and waste is driven from the value stream, the Lean team's efforts at root cause analysis often take shape as "intelligent guesswork," characterized by experimentation

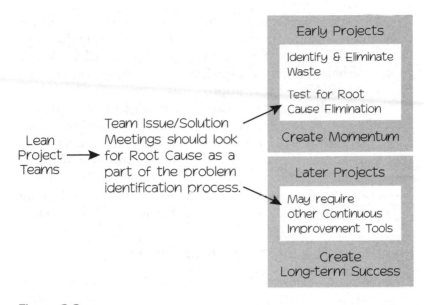

Figure 2-2.

and risk-taking. Although this is an important preliminary part of the Lean strategy, it should be seen only as a first step. Limits must be set for this type of Lean improvement —do it quickly, evaluate the results, and if the change is not successful, try another solution.

19

Value Stream Mapping

It is important not to try to create a detailed and structured approach when first implementing Lean. At this stage, power lies in simplicity. This is where value stream mapping (VSM) comes into play. A process mapping technique, VSM allows a team to create a visual template of what they need to know (and see) about an existing situation (or current state) to eliminate waste and improve a process. A good value stream map contains the following information:

- Process flow
- Information flow
- Employees in the flow
- Inventories and/or work in process
- Other pertinent data

This current state map gives the Lean team a "snapshot" of the value stream actually at a precise moment in time. Using this snapshot, the team can then create a future state map that reflects desired changes or improvements. Figures 2-3 and 2-4 show examples of a current state and future state map.

Team members interpret the maps through preconceived ideas about the process, focusing on what they think is most important. Using the VSM exercise as a basic framework and the future state map as a guideline, the team can begin to address opportunities for improvement. The maps and specified boundaries will keep change efforts *focused* on the opportunities identified. This prevents the team from getting distracted or going off on tangents or other crusades.

Identifying the Eight Types of Waste

All companies are affected by waste in one form or another. This chapter focuses on the eight most common varieties of waste. Commonly defined as the "Eight Wastes," these can occur sequentially or simultaneously.

20

1. **Overproduction.** Making or processing *more* than is required by the next step in the process; making or processing *earlier* than is required; or making or processing faster than is required.
2. **Excess Inventory.** Any supply in excess of the absolute minimum requirement to meet customer demand.
3. **Unnecessary Processing.** Any effort that adds no value to the product or service from the customer's point of view.
4. **Unnecessary or Excess Motion.** Any movement of product or machine, or employee movement that does not add value (as defined by the customer) to the product or service.
5. **Excess Travel.** The unnecessary or excess travel or movement of people, product, forms, or parts throughout a facility or organization.
6. **Defects.** Any type of undesired result is a defect. A failure to meet one of the acceptance criteria of your customers.
7. **Underutilized Employees.** Not using your employees' mental, creative, and physical abilities to their full potential.
8. **Waiting.** Time spent waiting for anything is a waste.

Each of these waste categories applies to manufacturing processes, service processes, and management/administrative processes. How you identify and eliminate waste may vary within the process, but the categories are always a valid way to group the wastes in your organization. Manufacturing products may be the easiest environment in which to understand Lean-model waste, because this is the primary setting for Lean discussion, implementation, and written materials.

In contrast, in the service sector, processes and even process tasks can vary greatly, depending on the industry and the organization's strategic goals, because the service sector includes such diverse organizations as healthcare facilities, schools and universities, repair and service centers, mortgage processing companies, banks, hotels, retail, etc. Service areas and transactional processes within manufacturing companies—such as sales, accounting, engineering, facilities management, and customer service—also experience this wide variation in process and task.

Management and administrative processes exist within every organization. From human resource departments to engineering, accounting, sales, and marketing departments, all management/administrative processes have Lean potential. The trick to applying Lean within these processes lies in convincing the employees of the following:

1. They have processes
2. There are non–value–added tasks
3. Employees can make a difference in simplifying and improving their processes.

Lean Methodology Strategy

The basic approach to get from *waste identification to waste elimination* is straightforward, regardless of the process type or sector. The difficulty comes from not following a Lean methodology. A typical Lean methodology strategy is summarized in Figure 2-6 on page 25, and each stage of this methodology is described in detail in the following sections.

CURRENT STATE MAP

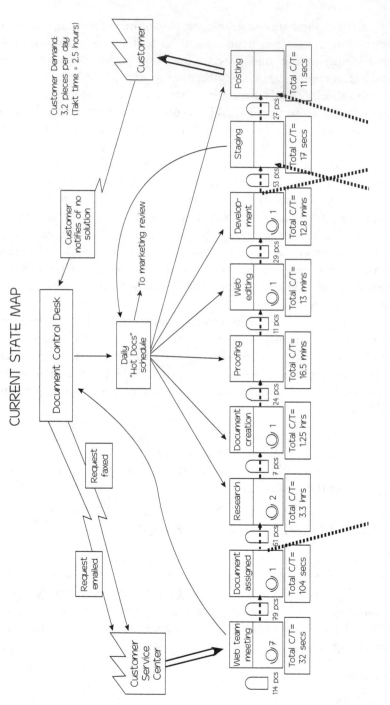

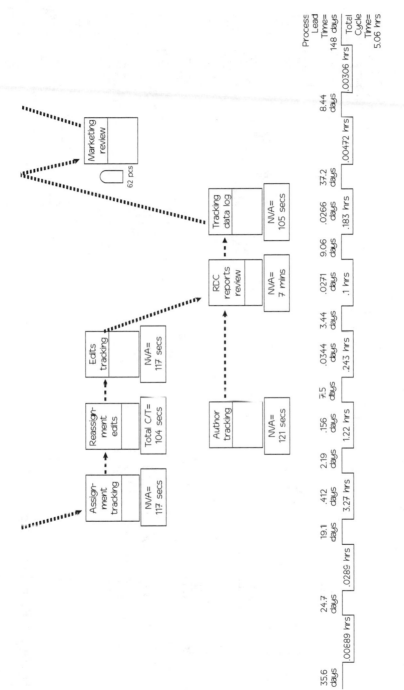

Figure 2-3. Current State Map

FUTURE STATE MAP

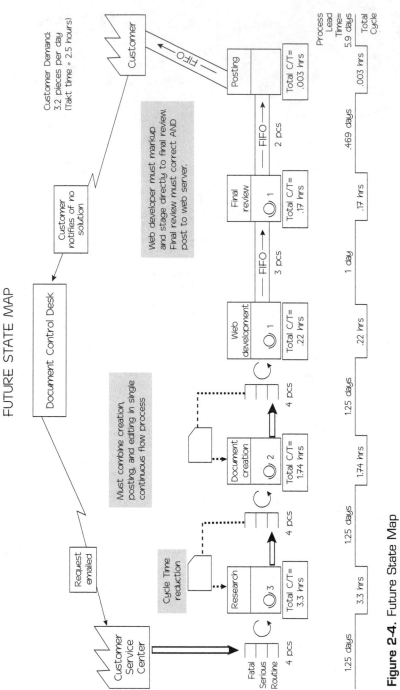

Figure 2-4. Future State Map

All organizations have support services, suppliers, and customers, just as manufacturers do. The difference is the Lean core, the primary product or service provided by the organizations.

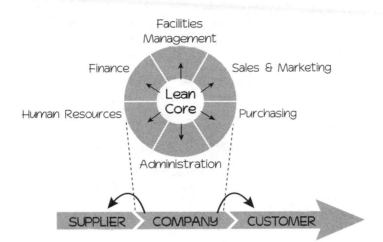

Figure 2-5.

Opportunity Identification	Solution Design	Implementation	Continuous Improvement
STAGE 1 →	STAGE 2 →	STAGE 3 →	STAGE 4
• Company-wide Diagnostic • Create a Common Understanding • Concepts Training • Understanding Value	• Value Stream Mapping • 5S System Development • Implementation Planning	• Pilot Projects • Phased Rollout • Ongoing Reprioritization	• Performance Measurement • Strategic Alignment

Figure 2-6. A Typical Lean Methodology Strategy

Stage One: Opportunity Identification

Stage One prepares the organization for entering the Lean world. You must:

- identify what opportunities exist,
- create a common understanding of Lean throughout the organization through team meetings and training,
- understand "value" as it is defined by the customer.

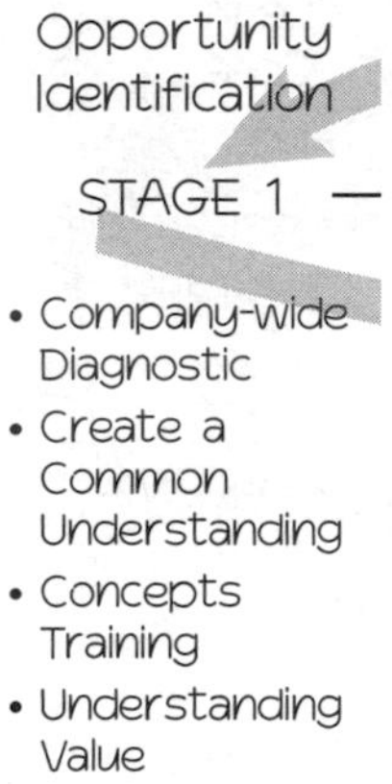

Opportunity
Identification

STAGE 1 —

- Company-wide
  Diagnostic
- Create a
  Common
  Understanding
- Concepts
  Training
- Understanding
  Value

26

Figure 2.7. A Typical Lean Methodology Strategy—Stage One

For Lean to be successful, all employees must be involved. This means that a common understanding of the concepts of Lean must exist within the workforce. In fact, this need for a common understanding of Lean must be an integral part of any type of initiative during the start up phase of any improvement effort. Lean overview or introductory classes and seminars are a good way to quickly create a common understanding of Lean. (Note that building a common understanding of Lean is dramatically different from Six Sigma training, which typically consists of very concentrated and detailed training sessions for a select group of participants.)

It is important to remember that creating an environment with a common understanding of Lean does not end with an introduction or overview. It is an ongoing process that depends on continuous reinforcement. Many organizations commit to Lean and then find that they must spread the training phase out over many months to keep processes moving. Some abandon their Lean journey during this training period, refocusing their attention on fire fighting or changes in management strategies. Organizations that stay the course succeed; they often realize a change in culture, become proactive in addressing problems and opportunities, or at the very least, gain a workforce that is open to try Lean improvements.

The true significance of this common understanding reveals itself when Lean projects, or *kaizen* events, are initiated. Lean teams, comprising employees working within the process and employees working "outside" the process, identify the issues and opportunities for improvement. For many employees, this problem–identification or brainstorming session is the first opportunity they have ever had to openly discuss their process problems, issues, or potential opportunities.

Brief team meetings encourage everyone to participate and assist in Lean improvements. Participants create a target list, and the core project team refines the list by reviewing the priorities identified during a value stream mapping exercise. From this priority list, the team can then start attacking "low-hanging fruit" and implement other solutions to eliminate waste. For the core team to be successful, it must communicate its plans and goals to, and invite input from, all employees working within the value stream.

The overarching message here is that project team members do not work in isolation; instead, they encourage all employees to help in implementing change. This worker-involved approach is extremely powerful because it allows employees to see their suggested solutions get implemented. This is especially important if a solution does not produce anticipated results. For employees involved in the process, this almost invariably becomes a matter of pride and they will work vigorously with the core team to modify the solution or identify another solution. The buy-in and continued involvement of employees is an invaluable asset to the project team and the company as a whole.

Stage Two: Solution Design

Stage Two is the foundational step of all Lean work. Documenting the current state and developing a future or goal state with value stream maps provide hard-copy, easy-to-understand process data that allows all employees to comprehend why Lean activity is being conducted.

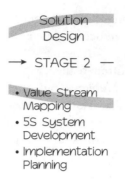

Figure 2-8. A Typical Lean Methodology Strategy—Stage Two

Many companies find that changing the culture to eliminate clutter and promote order can be facilitated by implementing a 5S organizational and housekeeping system—the 5Ss are *sort, set in order, shine, standardize,* and *sustain.* This gives employees the opportunity to use and maintain many Lean tools very quickly and create rapid improvements that visually and tangibly demonstrate the power of Lean. Successful 5S efforts are instrumental in changing the culture of an organization. However, it should be understood that many organizations start up 5S systems multiple times before it actually takes hold.

This stage also includes an implementation planning component. Using VSM in conjunction with Lean pilot projects moves the Lean effort forward at a rapid pace. Although this planning step is extremely critical, it generally takes only two to three days at the beginning of a project. This abbreviated planning time may go against the grain of most traditional process improvement efforts, but it is extremely powerful and sets the stage for proper implementation.

Because Lean relies on full employee participation in the improvement effort, many of the issues addressed in Lean rapid improvement projects focus on easy, "in your face" problems or "low-hanging fruit." By allowing team members to pick action plan items to work on, the first "pilot" items to be addressed are typically those things that the employees themselves view as major issues, whether management believes they are or not. Management must not discount this approach to continuous improvement. Allowing employees to deal with some "low-hanging fruit" early in the project life cycle engages them fully and quickly; it develops buy-in for both the project and the process almost immediately.

Every time a team removes "low-hanging fruit" from the list of problems or wastes identified within a value stream, it becomes easier to focus on the root cause. By peeling away the layers of symptoms causing waste, a team can quickly start seeing what remains of the problem. A variety of root cause analysis tools can then be used to help the team find the underlying issues and take corrective action.

Elimination of "low-hanging fruit" also sets the stage for dealing with more complex problems. Repeated attacks upon these more difficult problems will slowly squeeze as much waste from the process as possible. The overall skill and dedication of employees will determine how far an organization can go with Lean on these more complex issues. Although not all problems get resolved using Lean techniques and root cause analysis tools, it is a very rapid and effective way to eliminate waste and set the stage for future, more complex continuous improvement efforts. Quickly eliminating the easy issues through Lean also clears the way for Six Sigma tools to work much more effectively and more rapidly within the Six Sigma project cycle.

Stage Three: Implementation

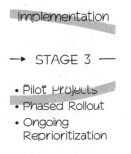

Implementation

→ STAGE 3 —

• Pilot Projects
• Phased Rollout
• Ongoing
  Reprioritization

Figure 2-9. A Typical Lean Methodology Strategy—Stage Three

Stage Three allows for a structured methodology of project work. During the startup phase of Lean, an organization will want to concentrate on small pilot projects that are easily achieved, controlled, and monitored. As successes are realized and seen by the workforce, a phased rollout of more projects can be implemented. The most dangerous pitfall associated with this phased rollout is starting and running more projects than can be controlled. As projects are finished, any remaining projects and/or areas of opportunity should be reassessed and reprioritized.

As the business world around us changes, we must react and continually determine where to go next, based on critical criteria developed by the organization. Sometimes, the direction is related to financial gains; more frequently, this prioritization strategy is based on ease of success, the amount of "pain" being experienced, improved service to the customer, or other similar factors.

Stage Four: Continuous Improvement

Stage Four begins a process of maintaining and sustaining the changes made, monitoring through performance measurement, and looking around at the organization as a whole to determine how the improvement efforts fit within the strategic plan of the organization. As results of these efforts become evident, attention can be shifted to another focus area or to additional changes to the same area.

30

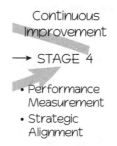

Continuous
Improvement

→ STAGE 4

• Performance
  Measurement
• Strategic
  Alignment

Figure 2-10. A Typical Lean Methodology Strategy—Stage Four

Either way, the cycle starts over. In fact, once you enter the Lean world, the cycle of continuous improvement never ends. If you let the initiative die, your workforce will perceive the entire effort as another "flavor of the month." If you keep the momentum going, the possibilities and benefits are endless.

Case Study #1: Adopting the Lean Philosophy at a Seat Belt Manufacturer

The speed at which significant results can be obtained through Lean is no more evident than at Beam's Industries, Inc. Beam's manufactures high-quality seat belt assemblies for diverse industries worldwide. These assemblies are used in (but not limited to):

- Amusement seating
- Classic cars
- School buses
- Agricultural/lawn products
- Medical equipment
- Emergency vehicles
- Automotive aftermarket
- Shuttle vans
- Van conversion
- Heavy trucks
- Military vehicles

After an extended period of sustained growth, management began to look for ways to keep the company moving forward, even during the economic downturn in 2002 and 2003. Beam's current president, Mike Bosley, who was director of operations at that time, realized that there were many opportunities for improvement within the company, notwithstanding the problems that were having a negative impact on U.S. manufacturing. Bosley was determined to keep Beam's an industry leader that would not succumb to the temptation of sending the work overseas just to cut costs as many other U.S. manufacturing facilities were doing.

Although the number of orders continued to increase, Bosley and the Beam's management team were vigilant about keeping ahead of their competitors, realizing that if the competition's market position improved, Beam's might find it difficult to retain its existing customers. Bosley identified the following problems:

- Lead times had begun to slip and were approaching eight-plus weeks.

- Uneven scheduling and customer delivery demands were causing large swings in the amount of work released to the production floor.
- These swings created periods of low work volume, followed by costly overtime.
- By visually analyzing the production floor, the management team realized that employees were lost among the mountains of work-in-process (WIP), raw materials, and finished goods waiting for shipment.

Management understood that Beam's competition had the ability to encroach on Beam's market share by offering lower pricing and similar delivery lead times. Management therefore recognized that Beam's competitive advantage rested within the "Value Proposition." As Bosley observed:

"We knew our advantage in the marketplace was in our high quality and ability to deliver on time at a fair price. We knew that we had to become more efficient before our lead times extended to a point where we would lose business. We recognized that we had a perfect opportunity to react. Being able to implement continuous improvement as a part of our culture gave us the incentive to keep our growth moving forward, before pricing and delivery issues could start having a negative impact."

This was the defining moment when the company decided to begin its Lean journey.

Using a balanced set of training and coaching, including training events and *kaizen*, Beam's began the Lean cultural change. Sending all employees through an introductory Lean class was critical to set the stage for changing the cultural mindset of the workforce. Management knew that a common understanding of the goals and objectives for change was critical in achieving employee support.

On-site training events, focusing primarily on value stream mapping workshops, were utilized to teach select staff how to use Lean tools. On-site, multi-day training workshops were preferred over off-site training, because the employees could learn Lean concepts using their own processes at the worksite. An additional advantage of this format was that at the end of the training, process improvement was either already planned or implemented.

Lean rapid improvement projects drove home the organizational message of change and commitment to Lean. Using outside facilitation was critical, because the fast-paced methodology of *kaizen* was completely new to Beam's.

Before long, every employee in the company became acutely aware that this was not the same company that had been doing business the same way for the past fifty years. Still, as Bosley put it, "Our management mindset had to change first, and this was not an easy task. Prior thinking was focused entirely on 'point utilization,' where every sewing machine needed to be running all the time regardless of demand or downstream pull."

Beam's started by reconfiguring one product line into a work cell. Company employees and management were impressed by the efficiency of the changes. The concepts implemented in the first cell were systematically transferred to other cells over eighteen months, and the increased throughput became readily apparent. Bosley concludes his explanation of Beam's Lean transformation with this comment:

> "5S remains a real need. We are leaner but still cluttered more than we should be. Lean helped us reduce lead times indirectly by helping us more accurately and quickly increase capacity in a very short time frame, usually about a week or less. All the things required to get Lean have made other aspects of our business much better, like determining labor costs, increasing capacity in a controlled way, HUGE improvements in quality, better supervision, etc."

Management was still concerned, however, that these changes on the manufacturing floor were not producing the overall results they had hoped for. For example:

- The number of orders taken was not increasing as expected.
- Revenue was not increasing as Bosley and other members of the management team had envisioned, even though the bottom line was improving.

It wasn't until outside facilitators conducted a Lean training event in the sales and customer service office that the most significant breakthrough moment occurred. Bosley summed up this progress:

"When we realized that we were still taking and processing orders the way we had always done it, we had one of those flat-head moments. The production floor was primed and ready, just waiting on more orders to flow to the floor. We had ignored doing Lean things with our *transactional* processes."

Since then, changes have been made throughout the organization. Employees have seen the results, and the culture of the company has evolved into one of almost total acceptance. "Our employees are more involved in the process and appreciate the opportunity to help improve efficiency. They are thinking outside the box ... literally."

In less than three years, Beam's has experienced the following results:

- 95 percent reduction in work in process
- 35 percent reduction in manufacturing floor space requirements
- 70 percent reduction in process lead time
- 25 percent increase in top-line growth

This last measurement has been critical to Beam's during its quest to respond to the "voice of the customer." Reducing delivery lead times from eight-plus weeks to less than two weeks positions Beam's at the top of its industry. It now has a competitive advantage and can meet the expectations of its customers specifications, delivery, and pricing.

But Beam's is not satisfied with its accomplishments to date on its Lean journey. Bosley notes:

"As we continue to develop new products and find new solutions for our customers, we must also continue to strive for perfection. We must continually look for a better, more efficient, and more cost-effective way to produce our products. Our employees understand this. And although management will provide the time, training, and tools to be successful, it is a company effort that is truly being led by our employees."

Conclusion

This chapter reviewed the purpose of Lean; explained the four stages of Lean to implementation, and offered a case study illustrating one manufacturing company's successful conversion to Lean. Chapter 3 describes the purpose and implementation of Six Sigma and includes a similar case study to illustrate how it can be used successfully.

The Power
and Focus of
Six Sigma

> We want to be not just better in quality, but a company 10,000 times better than its competitors. . . . We want to change the competitive landscape by being not just better than our competitors, but by taking quality to a whole new level. We want to make our quality so special, so valuable to our customers, so important to their success that our products become the only real value choice.
>
> JACK WELCH

Jack Welch did not jump on Motorola's Six Sigma bandwagon because he was looking for the latest and greatest business management philosophy. Welch was looking for a way to change the very heart and soul of GE. He was also looking for a way to improve GE's market position through quality and customer satisfaction that would propel the company to number one status. Welch believed that Six Sigma could help GE achieve both of these goals, and it is within this context that this work addresses the basic tenets of Six Sigma.

Six Sigma's Goal is to Eliminate Defects

Six Sigma is a process improvement initiative used to drive defects from processes. The goal is to create near perfection through continuous improvement that aligns "the voice of the process" with "the voice of the customer." No more than 3.4 defects per one million opportunities (DPMO) is the goal of Six Sigma level of quality (see Fig. 3-1). That ratio of success exceeds the success rate of nearly all current hospital processes in the United States. It is also a better record than telephone companies currently experience for dropped calls. With very few exceptions, it is better than any success rate that just about any organization in the world today can report. What makes this DPMO goal a great challenge is that it requires vigilance and diligence. Even the most exceptional organizations can slip from the lofty Six Sigma level, if they do not continuously look at their processes and improve them on a daily basis.

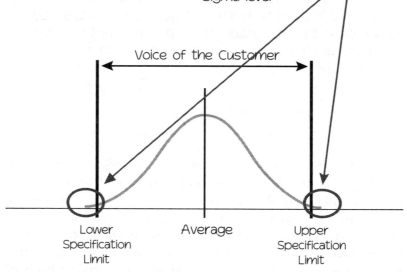

6σ=3.4 DPMO

The extremely small percentage of data points outside the specification limits shows where defects are found at the Six Sigma level

Voice of the Customer

Lower Specification Limit   Average   Upper Specification Limit

Figure 3-1.

38

A Brief History: Six Sigma at Motorola

Six Sigma as a process improvement initiative emerged from Motorola's desire in 1985 to reduce the number of defects within its processes. The ultimate goal was to achieve a significant reduction in the number of defects that fall outside six standard deviations of the upper or lower specification limit to 3.4 or less per million opportunities. Motorola recognized that fixing individual defects would, at best, yield a ratio of 6,210 defects per million opportunities (see Fig. 3-2). Motorola management also realized that reducing this defect number to 3.4 DPMO meant focusing the company's efforts on the *process* not the *individual defect*. The results were outstanding, and Six Sigma spread to other manufacturing and service organizations, with the most visible implementation being at GE under the watchful eye of CEO Jack Welch.

6.0	3.4
5.0	233.0
4.0	6,210.0
3.0	66,807.0
2.0	308,538.0
1.0	691,462.0
0.0	933,193.0

Figure 3-2. Sigma Levels

39

Like Lean, Six Sigma uses the "value proposition" to establish the strategic alignment of the voice of the process with the voice of the customer (see Fig. 3-3). In other words, any business that wants to achieve the highest profits possible must understand and meet or exceed customer expectations. Customer expectations include highest quality and lowest possible cost. To meet these expectations, and to retain and gain customers and increase sales and profitability, businesses must eliminate as many non-value-added tasks and defects as possible from the process.

Aligning the **Voice of the** Process within the **Voice** of the Customer is the goal to satisfying the Value Proposition.

Keeping your natural process limits inside your customers' specifications helps you to meet/exceed customer expectations.

To accomplish this goal successfully, you MUST remove as many non-value-added tasks as possible.

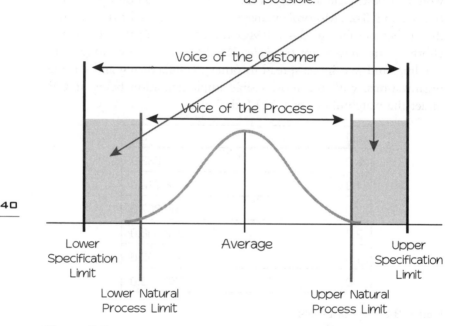

Voice of the Customer

Voice of the Process

Lower Specification Limit

Average

Upper Specification Limit

Lower Natural Process Limit

Upper Natural Process Limit

Figure 3-3.

Six Sigma's Structure and Improvement Methodology

A complex and statistically based initiative, Six Sigma has considerably more formal structure than Lean. Whereas Lean methodology has a relatively simple structure, which coordinates the activities of a champion, a *sensei*, a facilitator, and all employees, Six Sigma methodology is stratified into formal levels of knowledge. The Six Sigma structure includes the following hierarchy:

- Strategic council
- Business unit lead teams
- Champions
- Black belts
- Green belts
- Project teams

While the structure of Six Sigma is much more detailed than that of Lean and layered with additional levels of expertise and oversight, it is still continuous improvement, as shown by the similarities in the charts above.

Figure 3-4.

41

Another difference is that Lean relies on the basic Shewhart Cycle: *Plan, Do, Check, Act* (PDCA). In contrast, Six Sigma projects follow a more detailed process improvement cycle called the DMAIC Model (see Figs. 3-4, 3-5). DMAIC is an acronym for *Define, Measure, Analyze, Improve,* and *Control*. It was created to ensure that a systematic approach is always followed for positive and consistent results. The two cycles are similar, but each phase of the DMAIC cycle utilizes the PDCA cycle within it.

In the define phase, the strategic council submits a project to the champion. The champion and black belt further define the parameters, goals, scope, etc. of the project. The project is agreed on by

DEFINE	MEASURE	ANALYZE	IMPROVE	CONTROL
Establish definitive and recognizable boundaries for the project after concluding it meets the guidelines for a Six Sigma project.		Utilize data to identify predictability, variabilty, and opportunity for improvement by isolating key factors that effect these data and CTQs.		The mechanism to ensure that process improvements are implemented in a permanent and sustainable system.

| | Collect measurements of appropriate items that relate directly or indirectly to CTQs, allowing insight into what is really happening with the process. | | Make the process better. Drive your process from the current state to a new level by achieving goals of the project charter and reducing defects. | |

Figure 3-5.

the champion and black belt. The project team, in turn, must sign off on the goals and objectives of the project. This is accomplished through the creation of a *project charter*, which provides the following:

- the case for action
- a definition of the process
- an assigned champion
- a black belt assigned to manage the project
- the objective(s)
- the expected cost savings
- the team members
- the project scope
- the benefits
- the support required
- expected communications
- potential barriers and roadblocks

This information is formally documented in the charter and then signed by the champion, black belt, and all team members. It is then approved by the business unit lead team and the strategic council (see Fig. 3-6). Although this may seem like a convoluted and time-consuming way to launch a project, the results are worth the effort. Many Six Sigma (and other) projects have failed because they did not incorporate this upfront planning and focus. Because Six Sigma projects deal with multiple issues and defects within a single process, this chartering concept helps the project team work within set boundaries and avoid project scope creep (i.e., going beyond the boundaries of the original project).

To streamline the chartering process as much as possible, Six Sigma relies on a formal decision-making process for determining "what is" and "what is not" a Six Sigma project. Here again, it is important to note the distinction (as well as the connection) between Six Sigma and Lean. Although there are numerous strategies available for project selection, there are two basic philosophies that can be rapidly applied—regardless of which type of methodology you are using. In an organization relying on both Lean and Six Sigma, the purpose and strategies behind both methodologies must be understood:

- "Low-hanging fruit" and other basic waste-oriented opportunities are prime candidates for Lean projects.
- More complex issues that have had previous attention with little or no success often make excellent Six Sigma projects.

43

Although the chartering process is necessary for Six Sigma projects, it should be performed in as expeditious a manner as possible without compromising results or the integrity of the Six Sigma initiative. Some organizations may accomplish this by using a small, informal, but tightly run, management structure with three or fewer members on the strategic council, relatively few but powerful champions, and a limited number of black belts. Some organizations (such as GE), however, have created large formalized management structures intended to keep the initiative on track. In a 1998 interview, Jack Welch responded to the criticism of too much bureaucracy involved with managing a Six Sigma initiative by saying: "I don't give a damn if we get a little bureaucracy as long as we get the results. If it bothers you, yell at it. Kick it. Scream at it. Break it!"[1] Welch is still not afraid to apply resources to this type of initiative as

---

1. *BusinessWeek*, June 1998

PROJECT CHARTER: REDUCE NOISE (AVERAGE AND VARIATION) IN MOTOR 6249

Project Rationale	**Strategic Rationale**
	• Motor 6249 is a relatively new, high-volume product that provides power to medical devices. This motor is critical to keeping the current customer and expanding the medical market.
	
	Tactical Rationale
	• In two locations, production is experiencing high test and rework time and costs, which decreases capacity, contributes to overtime, and generates quality issues.
	
	Key Drivers
	• Unless the noise is reduced, the customer will take their business elsewhere
		Goals and Benefits
		
		Project Goals
		• Reduce the average from 50 to 30 and the standard deviation from 5 to 3.
		
		Project Benefits
		• Operational
		  Less rework
		  Less testing
		  Increased capacity with same resources
		  Greater first pass yield
		• Financial
		  Save $480,000 in operations costs
		  Eliminate the potential with charge backs

Process/Scope	**Project Scope**
	• Motor 6249 at the Piedmont Plant
	
	Project Boundaries
	  No fundamental motor redesign
	  No money for equipment upgrades
	
	Process to Improve
	• Assembly of end caps, bearings, and shaft
		Milestones
		
		Project DMAIC Timeline
		
		Phase Completion Date
		Define January 2006
		Measure February 2006
		Analyze March 2006
		Improve May 2006
		Control June 2006

Team	Champion: Sandra Dennis
	Black Belt: Harvey Ellis
		Members: Ron Early PE
		    Amy Austin, PE
		    Russel Martin, QE
		    Guy Thomas, OP
			Time Requirements: Black Belt-50%; Members-25%
			Meeting Frequency: Twice a week
			Meeting Location: Engineering Classroom

Figure 3-6. Charter Example

long as dramatic results, like those experienced at GE, continue to occur. According to Welch, if the Six Sigma bureaucracy becomes a problem, Six Sigma techniques can be used to improve it—just as it improves other processes.

Create Predictable Processes and Reduce Variation

Welch's position on this structure is at least partially based on the fact that improved processes that meet or exceed customer expectations means *improved profitability* (see Fig. 3-7). By focusing on the process, as opposed to an individual defect, it is possible to create stable and predictable processes. When processes are unpredictable, variation or other signals that something is awry soon become evident. It is then possible to identify and address the *root cause* of these variations or exceptions instead of simply fixing a *symptom*. After addressing the cause and creating a predictable or stable process, you can then address common causes of process variation.

Figure 3-7.

Six Sigma uses process behavior charts (or control charts, as they are more often called) to monitor processes and help identify routine noise versus signals within the process and assignable causes for specific issues that arise (see Fig. 3-8). By providing a picture of a process over time, these charts also provide insight into how a process is currently performing or behaving. Every action taken during this process provides the information necessary to make appropriate decisions regarding changes to improve the process.

Although many Six Sigma training organizations do not teach control charts until the "control" phase of belt training, Six Sigma works best when control charts are used as early as possible during

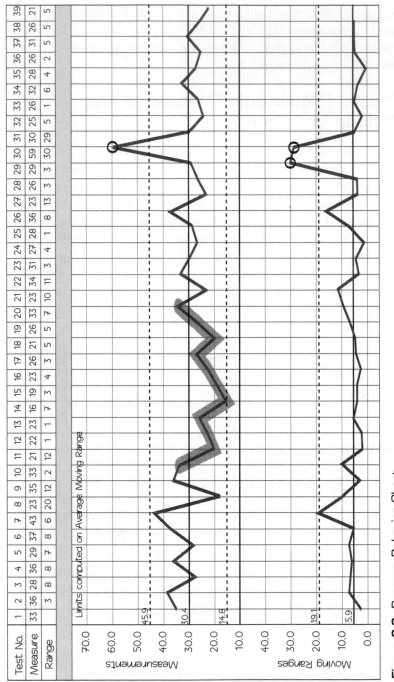

Figure 3-8. Process Behavior Chart

the measure and analyze phases. By establishing your critical-to-quality (CTQ) characteristics (as defined by the voice of the customer and translated into your process terms) early, and by beginning to measure these process tasks early, you can gain great insight into the overall process. By calculating the upper and lower limits of a process being measured with the predefined formulas on a control chart, it is much easier to understand what happens within the process naturally. The measurements and calculations can be used to identify all issues and opportunities of assignable or exceptional causes and eliminate them.

These items of assignable cause, which are exceptional variations in the process, become blips (i.e., signals) on the radar screen (i.e., control chart) to investigate. As long as exceptional variation occurs within the process, there is potential for defects and undesirable results, which may affect how the voice of the process responds or aligns with the voice of the customer. Many Six Sigma practitioners have begun using control charts as soon as a project is chartered and the CTQs are identified. This not only accelerates moving the project into the measure phase but provides useful knowledge about the capabilities of the process and differentiates exceptional variation that needs to be investigated from routine noise that is simply a normal result of the current process.

As items of assignable cause are removed or corrected, the process becomes more stable and predictable. With predictable processes in place, Six Sigma Black Belts can then begin to focus their efforts on the issues that are most important. Moreover, other Six Sigma tools can then be used as powerful weapons against the forces of evil—defects and variation. Design of Experiments (DOE), for example, can quickly assist in identifying root causes. The Six Sigma challenge then becomes how to implement the necessary changes required to eliminate or correct the defects. Once these have been eliminated, controls to ensure that the newly improved process is sustained can be brought into play.

Case Study #2: Using Six Sigma to Eliminate Defects at a Plastics Manufacturer

Six Sigma breakthroughs start with in-depth knowledge of the causes of variation in a process that lead to defects in the final product or service. For one manufacturer of molded plastic containers, the Six Sigma methodology was the key to removing defects in containers as well as improving the process efficiency.

A critical defect in the company's finished container was the thickness of two of the eight corners. These two corners were thinner than the other six; at times, they did not even meet the *minimum* thickness specification. The remedy initially used by production was to increase the total amount of material used to mold the containers. Unfortunately, this increase in material increased production cost. Moreover, it increased the weight of the containers, potentially compromising their internal capacity.

To launch the Six Sigma project, the manufacturer selected a process engineer to be trained as a Six Sigma black belt. After an intensive training course, the engineer worked with a champion to set up the project and select team members. During the course, the black belt had studied the DMAIC methodology, which he now applied to his project.

The define phase was critical to the project's success. Activities included the creation of a charter, which was used to keep the project on track. All team members, as well as the black belt and the champion, referred to the charter before considering any changes to the project scope. Additional activities focused on the major steps in the process that produced the containers and the critical-to-quality characteristics (CTQs) expected by the ultimate customer (i.e., the customer who purchased the product). The manufacturer decided to work on corner thickness because this was the major source of defects and cost.

Using the charter boundaries for the define phase, the Six Sigma project team constructed a process map and identified

48

measures for data collection. These measures included the CTQs as well as various process measures, such as temperature of the raw material when it is extruded and the extrusion pressure. The black belt helped the team set up data collection plans for all of the measures, and team members spent several weeks collecting data for the analyze phase.

During the analyze phase, the team analyzed the data, focusing on understanding the process and the causes of variation that might be associated with the corner thickness defects. The principle analysis tool used at this phase was a process behavior chart (i.e., a control chart), which identified the presence of exceptional variation as well as the amount of routine (i.e., common cause) variation in the process.

The team did not immediately rush to a solution, because its purpose at this juncture was to eliminate the causes of variation in the process. From the information on the various charts, the process team was able to find several causes of variation in the corner thickness for the problem corners and take actions to improve the thickness at these corners. Team members also identified several causes of variation that could improve the distribution of the raw material in the containers. They decided to conduct experiments with these causes of variation in the improve phase.

Conducting one-factor-at-a-time experiments was not new to the black belt, but performing experiments with multiple factors was. In the improve phase, the black belt used the techniques he learned in the course, and he led the project team in setting up a multifactor experiment on corner thickness. Specifically, the team goal was to learn how to

- reduce the corner thickness variation;
- reduce the total amount of material used;
- still meet the CTQs.

After two experiments, the team determined which factors in the process were responsible for the uneven distribution of material and proposed some process changes. The champion approved these process changes, and the team implemented them. After the changes were made, the team conducted additional experiments to determine the precise settings needed to achieve minimum material usage and still meet all specifications on corner thickness.

Once the team demonstrated that the process changes were successful in meeting the goals of the project, it moved to the control phase. During this phase, the team rewrote the process operating procedures and trained all operators in the new process. The team also set up a process behavior chart for critical measures to use in real time and response plans to assure that all signals of exceptional variation would receive prompt action. After a trial period, the project team turned the operation back to the champion and the operators. This project brought a $500,000+ savings to the company during the first year it was completed.

After the team members celebrated their success, the project team was disbanded. The manufacturer now had a trained Six Sigma black belt with one successful project completed and could initiate other projects as needed.

Conclusion

Chapter 2 reviewed Lean, and this chapter reviewed Six Sigma while pointing out a few of the distinct characteristics of each of these powerful methodologies. Chapter 4 takes a closer look at how Lean and Six Sigma compare and differ from each other.

LEAN AND SIX SIGMA ARE DIFFERENT INITIATIVES

It does not happen all at once.
There is no instant pudding.
DR. W. EDWARDS DEMING

Acknowledging that Lean and Six Sigma are different initiatives is critical to the success of an integrated Lean/Six Sigma effort. When organizations implement Lean Six Sigma, Lean Sigma® or some other combined effort, one discipline or the other can suffer or be compromised. The individual bias of managers controlling a single initiative where the autonomy of the methodologies is lost generally creates a power struggle between Lean and Six Sigma. Whichever discipline is "favored" by the controlling manager will win, and the other methodology will lose stature and may even fade from use.

This is not to say that the two initiatives should be managed totally separately. Although project teams should be allowed to operate without undue influence from management, it is prudent to have an executive council that strategically unites the two efforts. Project selection and review of results (see Fig. 4-1), as well as strategic use of the toolsets of each of the two methodologies, must be coordinated in a manner that precludes the struggle for resources and time throughout the organization.

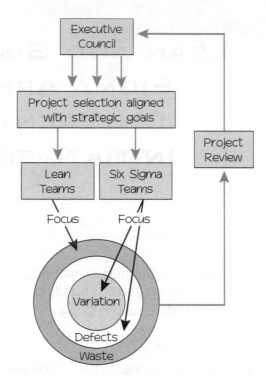

Figure 4-1.

Lean and Six Sigma: Focus on Different Aspects of Improvement

The focus of Lean is *to identify and eliminate waste through rapid implementation* of change designed to create pull systems in a continuous improvement environment (see Fig. 4-2). Through multiple passes (sometimes with trial and error), significant and immediate improvement is accomplished. Relying on the knowledge and skills of all employees and encouraging them to *participate actively* and *accept change* is the catalyst that keeps the Lean initiative on track and continually seeking out more opportunities to address. Many of the victories are little more than successful elimination of "low-hanging fruit," yet the cost savings and other metrics validate the power and potential of Lean.

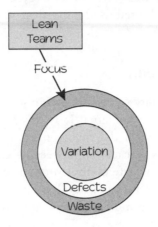

Figure 4-2.

On the other hand, Six Sigma focuses on re*ducing defects through the creation of predictable processes* with as little variation within those processes as possible (see Fig. 4-3). Six Sigma uses highly trained and skilled staff, master black belts, black belts, and green belts to determine the sources of defects and identify how a given process should

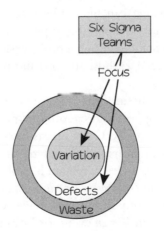

Figure 4-3.

operate to reach its maximum potential. The Six Sigma champions and belts (green and black) then work with all employees to adopt the changes and sustain the gains. Acceptance is essential, even though many of the rank-and-file employees will not understand the statistical approach used to identify the causes or be able to provide the answer(s) needed for change.

The Power of Lean

The speed and flexibility of Lean stands in stark contrast to the rigid structure required by Six Sigma. It is this fast-paced and flexible approach, partnered with the involvement of all employees, that drives Lean to success. Because employees are encouraged to recommend change and participate in implementing change, they accept it.

Detractors argue that Lean is too loosely structured, that it is not scientifically or engineering based, or that employees wind up with all the power. In truth, however, Lean project work is conducted within predetermined boundaries that keep project facilitators, team members, and employees focused on results. When implemented properly, Lean initiatives have little or no room to go astray.

The success of Lean depends on interaction with employees and speed (see Fig. 4-4). Often, the approach is to attack multiple areas in sequence or simultaneously within very tight parameters and with limited resources. This is possible because of the approach. A small Lean management team means that decisions can be made quickly and that change can be implemented nearly as fast. The momentum accomplished from this type of project methodology creates its own acceptance among employees. Positive results in a short time period breed enthusiasm and motivate people to make further improvements.

The underlying structures that support the management of the Lean initiative both support and encourage speed. Lean implementation rarely includes detailed Gantt charts or other Six Sigma project management tools normally used to manage and monitor progress. In the few instances when such tools are included in the Lean effort, there is almost always an understanding that the charts and lists must be constantly monitored, reviewed, and reprioritized based on the most recent *kaizen* event, or Lean project. Because the next step in a Lean transformation depends on the results of the

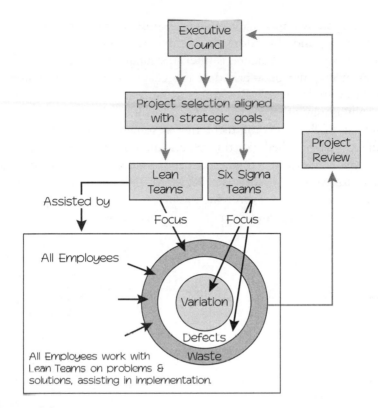

Figure 4-4.

most recent event, priorities change and are updated regularly as Lean teams review and understand the results of their work.

The term *kaizen* comes from Japan, where rapid, continuous, positive change is a cultural given, and the *kaizen* event (or "rapid improvement project") is the heart and soul of Lean improvement. Moving positive change forward at a fast pace is one of the factors that makes Lean so different from other continuous improvement initiatives. In many Lean transformations, early project events are sometimes described as *Kaikaku*, or radical change. During this early period of Lean transformation, many organizations make dramatic or even drastic changes in an effort to convince the workers within the process, managers, stockholders, or a combination of all of these that positive change is not only a good thing, but is necessary for the survival of the organization.

In Japan, when employees identify waste or other problems, the culture responds by addressing and correcting the situation as quickly as possible. Change is often instantaneous, and upper management may not be apprised of the change initiative until after it has been implemented. But whereas the Japanese culture embraces this philosophy of rapid change, it is difficult for the American company culturally to see the technique as something that truly works and can be controlled. For this reason, among others, many companies have "Americanized" the concept of *kaizen* by structuring it as three- to five-day "events" (see Fig. 4-5). This cultural nuance provides a comfort zone from which management and participants can more readily accept and direct a Lean transformation.

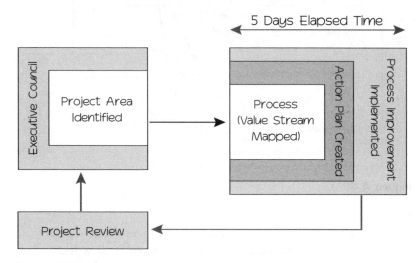

Figure 4-5.

Lean uses value stream mapping to document the current state and create a future or goal state. From these maps, the Lean project team can prioritize what, when, and where to work on waste elimination and process improvement. At the beginning of each *kaizen* event, the team should further document the current state by measuring critical factors that demonstrate that real positive change is being made during the three- to five-day project. At project end, these same metrics are measured again to show what has actually occurred.

When assessing the results of the event, the Lean team, along with the Lean champion and other management team members, can

56

review what transpired and determine the next step. This next step may be to conduct another event in the same area to generate even better results. It might be to address the next prioritized item on the action plan list created from the map sets, or it might be to reprioritize the action plan and add a new item that has appeared on the radar scope as a result of the just-completed event.

EVENT SCORECARD

Metric	Before	After	% Improvement
# pieces of paper generated	19	Avg. of 2.2	88.4%
Annual cost	$155,974.60	$12,623.90	91.9%
Travel path of work order	1,265 ft.	253 ft.	80.0%
Average # of touches	28	5	82.1%
Average age of work order waiting at assignment	24.1 days	2.6 days	89.2%
% of work orders submitted by e-mail	26.8%	91.1%	240.0%

Figure 4-6.

This fast-hitting, rapid, breakthrough approach to process improvement requires a considerable amount of faith in the Lean tools and technique. It also requires nearly as much faith in the workforce to do the right thing and a strong understanding of the *kaizen* methodology used to implement Lean. Organizations that are not comfortable with fast-paced change, or that have little experience in running improvement projects at a fast pace, may be wise to seek outside assistance in starting up such an initiative.

The Power of Six Sigma

In comparison to Lean, Six Sigma is a very structured and methodical continuous improvement concept that relies on its structure to ensure that strong, positive results are obtained through the project life cycle (see Fig. 4-7). Six Sigma requires much more management involvement than Lean, but the results can be equally dramatic. Organizations that pursue Six Sigma must realize the upfront cost requirements to build a Six Sigma structure and recognize that patience is an asset that can reap huge savings and additional benefits in the long run.

Everyone involved in building a Six Sigma structure (from the strategic council to the champions to the black belts and team members) must also understand the need for proper implementation of the methodology because this ensures that projects focus on the correct strategic issues and stay focused to generate improvements and cost savings. The decision-making process (as described in chapter 2) and charter creation alone can take thirty or more days. Aligning the goals and objectives of the project to the strategic goals of the

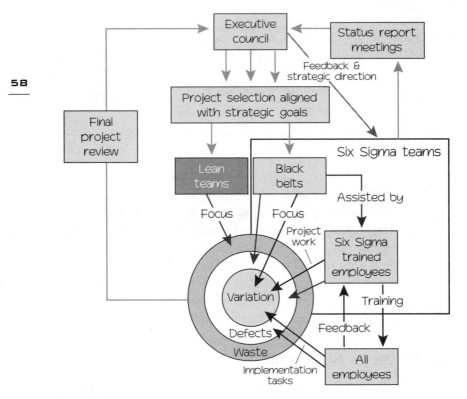

Figure 4-7.

organization is critical, because an average Six Sigma project may take four to six months to complete. If the effort is not focused on what is strategically important to the organization, and ultimately the customer, then this four- to six-month period has been wasted on non-value-added activity.

The average time required for a properly implemented Six Sigma project ranges from four months to one year from the start of project definition (see Fig. 4-8). (Project length should be targeted, however, to last no more than eight months even for the most complex projects.) The length of time required depends on the following factors:

- The complexity of the issues and opportunities addressed
- The time and support given to the project team to do the work
- The statistical process control (SPC) tools utilized during the project
- The organization's ability to understand the results and outcomes and to implement the required changes

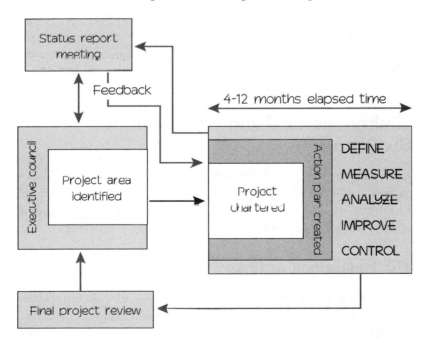

Figure 4-8.

During a Six Sigma project, the belts (both black and green), the project team, and ultimately the champion, drive and implement the bulk of the change. Data collection, analysis, decision-making, and implementation are the responsibility of the project team under the direction of the black belt. The black belt is accountable to the champion (and ultimately to the strategic council) for ensuring that the project is run successfully, which often means the black belt (along with the project team members) is the one making the change happen. Green belts and the project team conduct the day-to-day data analysis and process change.

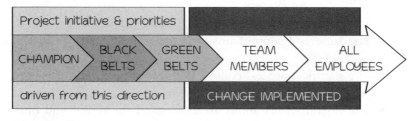

Figure 4-9.

Although the project team focuses on the project goals, the workforce as a whole needs to know what the outcomes are and why changes are being made. Only then will the changes be sustainable and adequately supported during future Six Sigma projects.

Limitations of Using Only Lean or Six Sigma

Lean and Six Sigma have supporters and detractors who are quick to point out what is right or wrong with one system or the other. Either approach, in fact, can be fascinating and financially rewarding at the end of the day; likewise, each has its own limitations.

The Limitations of Lean

Although it can produce incredible results, get all employees involved, and generate cultural change, Lean will eventually run into a problem that cannot be solved without more advanced statistical tools. Organizations that progress down the Lean path to the point that the return on investment (ROI) on project work diminishes over time to less-than-stellar levels, often find themselves looking for other methods of continuous improvement to squeeze out additional savings (see Fig. 4-10). Everyone, including management, knows an additional opportunity exists somewhere, yet Lean efforts continue to come up short in correcting the problem.

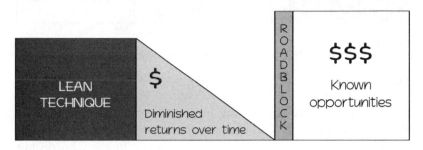

Figure 4-10.

Acceptance of the technique by the engineering community, finance departments, and upper management is also a potential limitation of Lean. Within many organizations, the numbers truly drive the direction of the company. These organizations cannot move forward on any project without traditional financial and/or engineering data and reports. If the Lean practitioner cannot find a data set that satisfies this requirement, other means of process improvement must be utilized.

The Limitations of Six Sigma

Six Sigma has its own limitations. The amount of time required to select, charter, and identify root causes and solutions often results in a substantial investment in labor dollars—which often leads to an ROI that is not sufficient to cover the cost of the project (see Fig. 4-11).

Moreover, because of the cost factor involved in managing and conducting Six Sigma projects, many smaller potential projects are overlooked because of the lack of sufficient ROI. Six Sigma is not designed for small projects. (The DMAIC methodology, however, can be used for projects of any size.)

Often, the lack of organization-wide employee involvement in Six Sigma projects results in "push-back" from the workforce (see

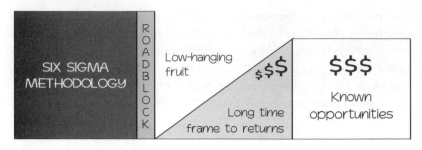

Figure 4-11.

Fig. 4-12). Because Six Sigma project work requires advanced skill sets from many team members, the average worker's role is to support the project by conducting business in the defined manner. When the results of project analysis are then explained, there can be a certain amount of skepticism from those employees who do not possess Six Sigma skills and/or knowledge. Because of the fear of change, this can then result in employees refusing to cooperate, or in a worst-case scenario, even sabotaging a project to ensure that the current way of running a process is unchanged.

62

One other problem that many Six Sigma project teams run into occurs during implementation planning. Although Six Sigma, when implemented properly, will most assuredly identify the causes of defects and variation and also show how the process should operate to avoid the defects and variation, it can be a struggle at times to identify how

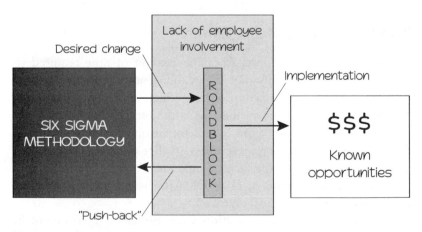

Figure 4-12.

to implement the changes needed to achieve project goals (see Fig. 4–13). Without proper techniques to implement process improvement in the project team's toolbox, changing the process can be difficult.

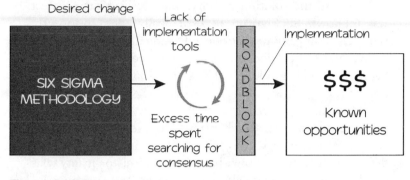

Figure 4-13.

This is a fairly common problem, and many Six Sigma project teams spend excessive time attempting to reach a consensus on how to implement the identified changes. Although Six Sigma provides all the statistical process control tools to identify the cause of problems and to show what a repeatable and defect-free future state could be, it does not always include a complete and precise methodology for implementation.

Case Study #3: Using Six Sigma to Eliminate Defects from a Paper Manufacturing Process

The bulk of a paper mill's product was sold to a customer who applied the paper to wallboard. Once the paper was applied, it was possible to see certain defects that were not visible prior to application. For some time, the customer and the paper mill had blamed each other for the defects. The customer said the paper itself was flawed; the paper mill said that the defects came from the customer's process of applying the paper to the wallboard. Because the customer represented more than 50 percent of the company's business, the burden of resolving this dispute lay with the paper mill. Unfortunately, the company did not step up to the challenge until the customer refused to buy any more paper.

Because the solution to what was creating these defects was unknown, Six Sigma tools were ideally suited to solve this issue. The company was introduced to the methodology of Six Sigma, and the production manager agreed to become a Six Sigma black belt and lead a team to work on the paper defect problem.

The define phase was relatively easy to complete because the paper process was already mapped, the scope of the project was clear, and the goal was to reduce the incidences of these defects and get the customer back. The critical-to-quality characteristics (CTQs) were also clear because the customer had defined them.

The major difficulty in the measure phase was that the defects did not show up until after the customer used the product. The paper mill had to simulate the customer's process and determine what measures of the paper would be related to the existence of the defects. There was a lot of data on numerous characteristics of the finished paper. Most of the existing data was used in the beginning of the analyze phase. Later, other measures were identified and studied.

During the analyze phase, the project team spent hours analyzing the data it had collected to determine what characteristics of the paper were related to the defects. At first, it appeared that none of the relationships they believed existed would help determine the causes of the defects. Finally, project team members started making process behavior charts with the time-ordered data—and the first thing they discovered was that the paper production process was not predictable. The charts revealed numerous instances of exceptional variation.

Using the process behavior charts, the project team began a concentrated effort to stabilize the paper production process. They still were not clear about which characteristics of the paper were critical to the defects, but they understood that the causes of exceptional variation were very clearly not beneficial.

As project team members eliminated one after another of the causes of the exceptional variation, the process ran more smoothly. The team set up in-house tests for the defects that the customer observed. These in-house tests indicated that the frequency of the defects was declining, and the overall quality of the paper was improving.

The activities of the improve phase focused on testing the changes to ascertain whether they would eliminate the causes of exceptional variation. At the same time, the paper mill managers contacted the customer and requested a meeting. During the meeting, the project team showed what actions they were taking and the improvement in the results. The customer agreed to take some paper on a trial basis.

Once the team knew exactly what changes were necessary, they moved to the control phase. During the control phase, the team updated some procedures and created additional procedures. They put control and response plans in place, using process behavior charts to ensure that any exceptional causes of variation would be discovered quickly and that appropriate actions would be taken to eliminate them.

After training all employees in the new procedures, the project team supervised a trial period of eight weeks to ensure that the process could maintain the new level of quality. During this period, the team also monitored the results at the customer's facility to make certain that the frequency and severity of the defects fell within the customer's acceptable range.

Six Sigma methodology was critical to regaining a customer who was lost by a lack of understanding of the sources of variation that caused defects. Ultimately, the success of this project led to other business as well.

As variability is removed from a process, the process becomes more predictable, and ultimately, quality is improved by eliminating the defects resulting from variation. The net result is increased bottom-line profitability. In addition, an increase in quality, as defined by the customer, generates greatly heightened customer satisfaction, which generates more sales and ultimately more profit. Just as with Lean, eliminating the things that are non-value-added to the process reduces costs and defects, allowing an organization to focus on the business goal within the value proposition: *to yield the highest possible profits*.

The skeptic may say that all this really does is reduce costs so that the sales force can charge less for a product or service. But as GE and Motorola have proven, dramatic improvements in process and quality actually create a competitive advantage not only to *maintain* but *improve* market share.

By running processes on-target with minimum variation, organizations are more capable of delivering virtually defect-free products and/or services much faster. High-quality products and service, combined with lower costs and faster delivery times, are what the customer expects. When an organization can deliver a product or service by moving the voice of the process into alignment with the voice of the customer by using continuous improvement initiatives such as Six Sigma, the value proposition is satisfied. Ultimately, what customers and competitors will see is a world-class, successful organization.

Case Study #4: Applying Lean When Six Sigma Tools Are More Applicable

Providing computer accessories to a very competitive market kept the management team of one electronics manufacturer constantly searching for ways to stay competitive and keep increasing market share. Although the company was in the early stages of a Six Sigma initiative, several facilities around the world were looking for faster ways to improve and reduce costs. A blend of concepts and ideas were being used at several locations. However, one manufacturing center focused its efforts specifically on Lean improvements.

This facility had undertaken several Lean projects when management finally selected two candidates (both manufacturing engineers) from the location to go through Six Sigma black belt training. During the second week of training (approximately six weeks into the training program) at the corporate offices, the local management team launched a new Lean project focused on quality and flow problems of one assembly line. During the first three weeks of Lean efforts, the Lean team assigned to the project quickly attacked several known issues. The action resulted in more than $75,000 in annual savings and freed up more than 9,000 square feet of floor space.

After four weeks of *kaizen* on the assembly line, spread over twelve weeks, the team had addressed more than 80 percent of the problems identified by the assembly line operators, engineers, and quality technicians. However, quality problems continued to plague the product family. Customer returns were growing, but there was no single failure point, or overwhelming customer complaint on which to focus quality improvement efforts. The Lean team continued to search for opportunities for improvement, but the cost savings and other Lean improvements were becoming proportionately smaller as the effort entered its eighth week.

Meeting with management during a quality progress meeting ten weeks after the Lean effort on this product line was initiated, the Lean team facilitator disclosed the frustration that the team was experiencing over the quality issues. The quality manager suggested that the problems (or defects) were most likely related to the plastic case that enclosed the product, but this was not corroborated by the samples reviewed in the quality lab. Although multiple failure points were discovered, all materials measured met specifications.

The black belt candidates suggested that the Lean project be converted to a Six Sigma project. Soon after, one of the new black belts met with the Lean team and quality manager to discuss the situation. At this meeting, everyone involved agreed that the problem most likely had something to do with the plastic case, because it was the single point of commonality in all returns. However, the precise point of failure varied greatly. In some cases, one screw hole was stripped out and plastic tabs were broken; in other instances, all the screw holes were stripped, but no tabs were broken. A wide variety of combinations of these problems also existed. Compounding the situation was the fact that the stated reasons for returns varied widely. Some were returned for a vibrating sound, others for loose cases or cords, and others for rattling noises.

Working together, the black belt, the quality manager, and the project champion developed a charter focused on these issues. A small project team consisting of the black belt, a quality engineer, a product engineer, and the line supervisor met with local management to explain the charter and their plan of attack. A control chart was established, and a random sample of completed units was inspected at the end of the line to look for failure points that had been overlooked to date.

After a week of sampling, it was apparent that something was causing screws to strip out the holes even though all screws measured met specifications. It was subsequently discovered that these defects appeared sporadically, but only during certain product runs. This led the team to start looking at the plastic itself and the torque drivers used to install the fasteners. Design of Experiments (DOE) was used to look at each torque driver when it was used on the line and the position where it was utilized.

Eventually, the team found four of twelve torque drivers were over-tightening screws. The defects were appearing only when these four (or any subset of the four) drivers were on the line. The team also discovered that these defective drivers were not being routinely used; they often remained on the tool rack adjacent to the line.

Following this discovery, a relatively simple experiment showed that these four drivers were also the cause of the loose cords. However, it took another set of experiments aimed at how operators were snapping together cases to find the cause of the broken tabs. One employee, improperly trained on the technique of snapping the two case pieces together, was the cause. Both the defect and cause had been hidden behind the rotation of staff from position to position on the line.

These quality issues might never have been discovered using Lean tools and techniques alone, because the speed and focus of Lean masked the problem. Once the problem no longer occurred, the Lean team would have assumed the problem was solved and moved on to other opportunities.

Conclusion

The purpose of this chapter was to highlight the differences between Lean and Six Sigma, from the perspective of structure and focus as well as function. Chapter 5 focuses on the importance of organizational culture and acceptance of Lean or Six Sigma methodology as criteria for success.

CHAPTER 5

CREATING THE CULTURE FOR SUCCESSFUL CHANGE

People work in the system.
Management creates the system.
—DR. W. EDWARDS DEMING

A simplified view of Deming's famous quote suggests that all a management team has to do is create a system and that employees will willingly work within whatever system management delivers. But many managers in today's business world would immediately pronounce this interpretation flawed because it ignores the fact that employees no longer just blindly follow "the boss." Their experience tells them that employees are living, breathing human beings with their own ideas about the way things should be. They don't always want to agree with or do what management wants them to do.

Paradoxically, and in spite of human nature, management-created and management-imposed systems are a reality in most businesses, and employees, regardless of what they may initially think, tend to adapt to whatever "system" management creates. If management creates a quality-based, goal-oriented, aggressive, and consistent approach to business that values the workforce's knowledge and

Figure 5-1.

skills, employees respond well—not overnight, but over time. Eventually, day by day, the new culture becomes part of the employees' routine.

This happens, to some extent, even if management fails to provide a consistent approach to conducting business. Employees may resist a change they perceive as just another "flavor of the month." Long-time employees in particular will view the latest and greatest ideas in process improvement as just another example of management not knowing what they are doing or where they are going. But rather than responding with outright challenges, employees respond through a variety of "wait and see" tactics.

It should be noted that even companies that don't subscribe to the philosophy of "process improvement" experience this reaction by their workforce. For example, think of the organizations that will not fire problem employees. Often, the decision not to fire someone is rationalized as "There's a long line of others just waiting to take his place. At least I know who the problem is today." Or what about the companies that "allow" employees to come to work late, take long lunches, or leave early with no adverse consequences? Whatever the situation is, the employee will adapt to it over time. In the scenario described above, they will adapt proactively. In the scenarios described here, they will adapt by taking advantage of management's ineffectiveness without fearing consequences: A culture has

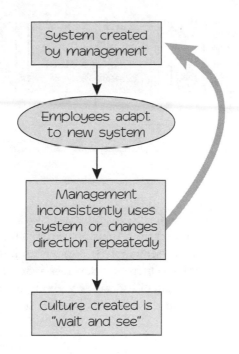

Figure 5-2.

been established, and employees know how to live and survive in this culture.

So the real question here is how to create a culture for successful change. What must management do to overcome bad habits and inconsistencies to implement positive change successfully within an organization?

Developing a strong cultural foundation based on Lean thinking is a start. Instilling a common understanding of Lean and teaching employees the reasons why all organizations need to make positive changes is critical. So is training them to utilize Lean tools and techniques.

Lean Thinking: Laying the Foundation for Cultural Change

Lean thinking is the cultural aspect of Lean that brings all employees of an organization together in a continuous search for better, more efficient ways to conduct business. Lean thinkers are always

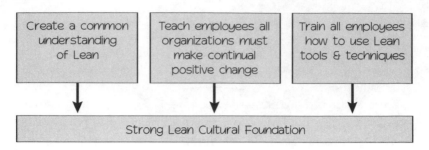

Figure 5-3.

striving for perfection and looking for ways to drive non-value added tasks (i.e., waste) from their processes. This means reacting to the pull of customers (see Fig. 5-4). Understanding that the best way to provide quality products and services is to respond when customers request a product or service by giving them what they want, when they want it, at the lowest possible cost.

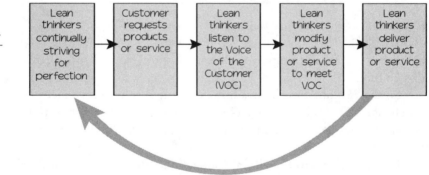

Figure 5-4.

Lean thinkers continuously improve their processes and routinely reevaluate even those processes that appear to be running problem free. This means creating and maintaining a culture that not only understands the need for continuous improvement but also proactively seeks opportunities to improve.

To create this culture, the organization must push the Lean concepts down from the top (see Fig. 5-5). Top-level management must be ever vigilant about reinforcing the decision to pursue perfection, encouraging all employees to participate, and changing or eliminating those employees (and managers and supervisors) who do not want to work in the Lean environment. Jack Welch's now-famous quote, "We will change the people or change the people," is as valid for Lean as it is for Six Sigma. You must create a Lean culture and truly make it "the" culture if you want to attain the level of success that Lean can deliver. Although Lean practitioners will tell you that one of the basic tenets of Lean is not to eliminate employees, most successful Lean practitioners will admit that changing the culture is difficult and that the difficulty is greatly compounded by those employees who refuse to change. The corollary to this is that if someone chooses not to change to fit the Lean culture, it is better to keep the culture than the person, regardless of the cost.

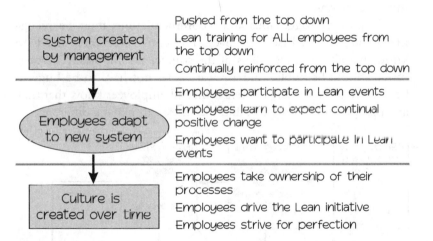

Figure 5-5.

To initiate cultural change to Lean thinking, an organization must start out by giving the entire workforce—from the lowest-paid employee all the way up to the CEO—some form of Lean training. Although many companies believe they cannot afford to hold a one-day class for each and every employee, the reality is that they cannot afford *not* to do this. Laying the proper Lean foundation requires conviction and investment. Upper management must subscribe to both if it wants to drive the organization to a Lean culture or the initiative will not succeed.

You can begin the process of creating a Lean culture through all-day, introductory Lean training sessions or through two- to four-hour overview sessions designed to provide a common understanding of the need to change and the power of Lean. This overview and the creation of common understanding are essential. Employees' questions must be answered. Their fears and concerns must be understood and addressed. For positive change to occur it must be desired and accepted and this means a shift in mindset.

The workforce as a whole must see the commitment of the executive management team to Lean, and this cannot be relegated to words in a vision statement. It has to be a real part of the organization's culture—day in and day out. Managers and supervisors must be held accountable for their actions, or more appropriately, their *inaction* when they are not maintaining and moving the Lean initiative forward.

Employees' suggestions and recommendations must be recognized and rewarded (see Fig. 5-6). The entire workforce needs to know that all ideas, regardless of the source, are important. Recognition should be public, and a reward does not have to be huge to be effective. What really matters is that all employees know that they are a part of the Lean effort and that they can make a difference.

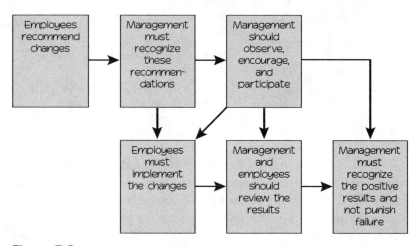

Figure 5-6.

Advanced Lean training and repetitive "rapid improvement events" within an area utilizing valid suggestions of employees reinforce the shift to a Lean culture. You cannot achieve this by simply *telling* the workforce that this is continuous improvement; you achieve it by *showing* and participating in training and events (see Fig. 5-7). By taking part in *training* sessions, by emphasizing the importance of training, and by participating in rapid improvement events, or *kaizen* events, management visibly and tangibly solidifies its commitment to Lean. At times, this means a down and dirty approach to management that shows employees just how strong the commitment to Lean truly is. Nothing can be more powerful and convincing for employees than the sight of a top-level manager on his or her hands and knees, scrubbing a floor or pulling trash from under a workstation.

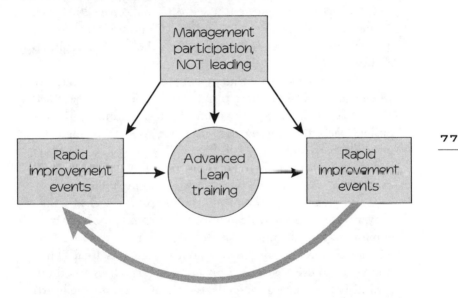

Figure 5-7.

Anything management can do to reinforce the commitment makes the message stronger and clearer to the workforce. And yes, sometimes this shift to Lean requires terminating an employee. Sometimes, the cultural change depends on removing a human roadblock from the organization. An employee who cannot or will not accept the cultural change is a threat; this person has the potential to derail or impede change and you should not hesitate to "change the person" by removing the roadblock and replacing him with an employee who understands the benefit of the change in culture. Doing this sends a very strong message that this is the "real deal" (not another flavor of the month) and that the rules have changed.

Case Study #5: A Lean Cultural Change at a Gear Manufacturer

Amarillo Chittom AirFlo and Amarillo Gear Company are members of the Marmon Group of Companies. The Marmon Group is an international association of more than 100 companies that operate independently within diverse business sectors. Collective revenues exceeded $6.3 billion in 2004. Bill Immell, general manager of Amarillo Chittom AirFlo (ACA), doesn't pull any punches when telling the story of cultural change at ACA:

"We had made several attempts to start up a Lean initiative when we were a family-owned and -operated business. Each and every time we discussed it, a group of our long-time employees pushed back, threatening to quit if we tried to change our processes. Each and every time, the employees won. Our culture had evolved to a point where the workforce didn't believe change was necessary and wasn't afraid of losing their jobs.

"On the eve of the company's sale to Amarillo Gear Company, my new boss and I found out that eight very long-time employees were planning on not showing up the next day when we were to announce that the sale was final. They wanted us to see that the company couldn't survive without them. My boss made a tough decision that won over the hearts of many of our good employees. He backed the decision to fire the employees who failed to show up the next day. He said that we would make it work without their help. A week later I rehired two of those employees who came to my office begging for their jobs. But old habits are hard to break. Neither one of those guys works for us today," Immell states very matter of factly.

When you tour the ACA facility today and see what Lean has done for the company, you quickly realize there is more than process improvement at work. You see a *cultural* change at work, too. During the tour, you will observe excellent examples of work cells, visual aids, and standardized work. But the *cultural awareness* becomes even more evident when you ask any employee about the many display boards seen throughout the plant. Every floor employee will explain in great detail what each metric means, how and what is being done with it, and what should be addressed next. Ask about *takt time*, and you will hear not only a near perfect definition but a precise statement about the status of current takt time. Ask about *kanbans* and expect to be directed across the floor where *kanban* cards are being used.

ACA has transformed its plant into a Lean facility. More importantly, it has changed the culture. It is producing more and has reduced its direct labor *cost* by roughly half of what it was before Lean was implemented. After the initial roadblock elimination, the only reductions in the labor *pool* have resulted from attrition. With material costs rising by up to 40 percent in some instances over the past three years, prices quoted to customers have not increased at all during this same time period. The company is now looking at growth and relishing the thought. Change is good. And no ACA employee thinks Lean is a "four-letter word."

Strategy-driven Six Sigma™: Laying the Foundation for Cultural Change

Introducing cultural change to a Six Sigma world is more difficult than doing so in a Lean world, but it is an attainable goal. Strategy-driven Six Sigma™ (SDSS), which focuses on the results, not just the Sigma level, can make this cultural change smoother and faster. SDSS is designed to be process focused and project enabled with the goal of defect-free output. Additionally, SDSS focuses on growing the top line while improving the bottom line and customer satisfaction (see Fig. 5-8). This approach is tied directly to the value proposition, which establishes that:

Businesses have a right to produce products and offer services that yield the highest-possible profits. Customers have a right to purchase the highest-quality products and receive the highest-quality services at their lowest-possible cost. The value proposition recognizes this alignment as critical to all improvement efforts.

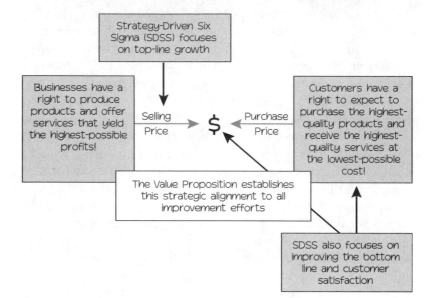

Figure 5-8.

By shifting the focus away from the Sigma level (i.e., the number of defects per million opportunities) as the primary goal of Six Sigma, it is possible to bring more employees into the continuous improvement effort by focusing on what is easier to understand— i.e., customer satisfaction and improved sales and profits. Again, this shifts the focus from some mystical number that is only understood by the belts, champions, and engineers. This is not to say that measuring and monitoring are not important. They are. But their value increases in direct proportion to the cultural changes that make them meaningful to the workforce. During the process of change, the workforce begins to understand what is happening and becomes a part of it. The workers must be involved in the change, identifying opportunities and tying potential projects to the strategic direction of the organization.

When this begins to happen, the workforce will more readily accept Six Sigma as a continuous improvement effort and be more accepting of change in general. The power of Six Sigma, utilizing the strategy-driven approach, allows for faster acceptance by the workforce, because workers are seeing and hearing about issues and opportunities that they understand and deem important (see Fig. 5-9). Because the SDSS initiative disseminates Six Sigma knowledge and fosters ongoing communication with the workforce, most employees are involved and see themselves as an integral part of the approach rather than as passive targets of another management-mandated system or process.

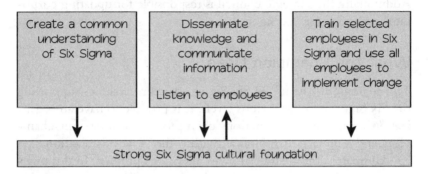

Figure 5-9.

Correctly establishing a strong Six Sigma foundation will also contribute greatly to the success of the initiative. The structure of the effort and how it is rolled out can help ensure that the Six Sigma approach is maintained long term. Six Sigma is a much more structured approach than Lean—to maintain the focus and level of effort required to get the answers to the difficult problems that Six Sigma addresses, it has to be. As noted in chapter 3, many opponents of Six Sigma attacked Jack Welch at GE over this formal structure and the added administrative work it brings to the table. Welch's response, also cited in chapter 3, is worth repeating in this context: "I don't give a damn if we get a little bureaucracy as long as we get the results. If it bothers you, yell at it. Kick it. Scream at it. Break it!"

In some ways, the structure of a Six Sigma organization (which includes a strategic council, champions, black belts, and project teams) is similar to the structure of Lean and many other continuous improvement efforts. What sets the Six Sigma structure apart is how these various components work and what happens at each step of any given project. It is within this structure that the list of all potential projects is kept.

What the Strategic Council Does

The strategic council maintains oversight of all Six Sigma projects and provides critical advice and approval of potential projects based on the strategic goals of the organization. The council also stays in regular contact with all organizational and business unit leaders. Additionally, the strategic council is responsible for updating corporate-level goals for Six Sigma.

What the Champion Does

The champion's role in the Six Sigma structure includes supporting the Six Sigma effort at various levels. It is possible to have an organization champion, an operations champion, a business unit champion, and a project champion all within the same organization.

Ultimately, the champion owns Six Sigma projects. In this ownership capacity, it is the champion's responsibility to keep moving the Six Sigma initiative forward by providing resources, removing roadblocks, supporting the development of and sustaining "statistical thinking," and working with black belts to ensure that they remain properly focused (see Fig. 5-10). Champions work to ensure

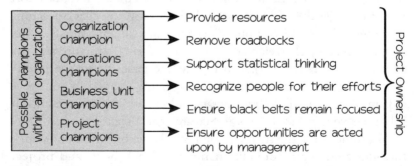

CHAMPIONS OWN SIX SIGMA PROJECTS

Figure 5-10.

that project opportunities are acted on by the organization's leadership and specifically by financial management. Last, but not least, champions recognize people for their efforts.

What the Black Belt Does

As shown in Figure 5-11, Six Sigma black belts function as project managers; they "run" the projects. What differentiates black belts from "normal" project managers is the specific and detailed knowledge of Six Sigma tools and concepts used to reduce defects, to identify causes of variation, and to use the Six Sigma DMAIC framework to move a Six Sigma project through its life cycle. A black belt leads and directs teams in the execution of projects.

BLACK BELTS MANAGE SIX SIGMA PROJECTS

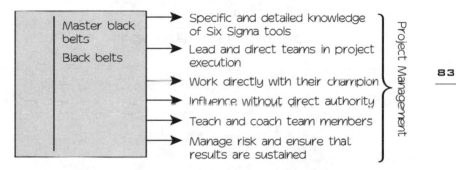

Figure 5-11.

The black belts work directly with their respective champions, soliciting their help when necessary and reporting progress. They must be able to influence without direct authority and must also be able to determine the most effective tools to utilize. This collaboration begins as soon as a potential project has been identified. Black belts and champions work together to define the project and formally document the information by using a project charter. Black belts must prepare a detailed project assessment during the measurement phase and are charged with soliciting input from knowledgeable operators, front-line supervisors, and team leaders. This input is essential because it ties into the desired cultural change.

Black belts are responsible for teaching and coaching the necessary tools and techniques to team members and workers within a project area. They must also manage project risk; after the fact, they must ensure that results are sustained.

What the Project Team Does

Finally, there is the project team, which has the most direct contact with frontline employees. This team, along with the black belt, is perceived as "the Six Sigma effort," both within the organization and among the organization's customers (see Fig. 5-12). Team members participate in project work within the context of their existing responsibilities. They are encouraged by the black belt and champions to the Six Sigma concepts and tools utilized on their project. After the completion of the project, team members are also encouraged to continue to use these tools and concepts and to learn additional Six Sigma skills for future team work.

PROJECT TEAMS "ARE SIX SIGMA"

84

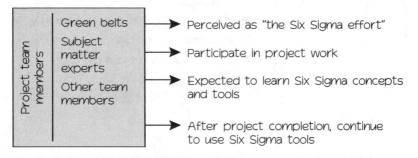

Figure 5-12.

How Strong Leadership Helps

Utilizing this detailed structural approach and implementing Six Sigma through SDSS, as opposed to just focusing on attaining a numeric Sigma level, it is possible to have great success with Six Sigma. It is also possible to change the culture through a very intense and dedicated effort by leadership to show employees that this is a top-down effort, it is continuous, and it will involve everyone through knowledge sharing and other communication throughout the workforce.

Case Study #6: A Six Sigma Cultural Change at a Cabinet Manufacturer

At the start of a Six Sigma initiative, a manufacturer of custom kitchen cabinets was receiving complaints about incomplete shipments from a home-improvement store. Because it was beginning a Six Sigma initiative, the company decided to work on this problem as its first project, following the standard DMAIC process: define, measure, analyze, improve, and control.

During the define phase, the company was able to complete a project charter and set goals for the project. Even though it was not completely certain of the process to be improved, it moved on to the next phase.

There was difficulty in collecting data on the incomplete shipments because the process required that the customer complete a form and return it to the manufacturer. However, the company did collect data and began to analyze it. Meanwhile, the black belt and project team members continued to work on a process map and determine just what process needed to be improved. They finally made an end-to-end process map, starting with the order from the customer and ending with the shipping of the ordered cabinets.

Once the end-to-end process map was in place, the team realized that the biggest reason for partial shipments could be traced back to the "kitting" process, which consisted of collecting all of the components for a cabinet order and forming a "kit" to send to assembly. Data showed that the number of kits sent to assembly with missing components was much higher than anyone suspected. The entire order for these cabinets could not be completed in assembly at the same time, and the result was incomplete shipments.

This phase focused on learning just how often incomplete kits were sent to assembly and which components were missing. Some of the errors in kitting were associated with parts in the wrong locations and selection of the wrong parts. By correlating visual information in the end-to-end process map and the statistical data, the team members realized that the causes of partial shipments could be traced back to the kitting process. They then began to consider fundamental changes to the kitting process that would eliminate the errors and the problem of incomplete kits going to the assembly process.

In this phase, the team brainstormed what changes could be made in kitting that would eliminate the errors and incomplete kits. Team members considered some far-reaching changes and experimented with several versions of change. After evaluating the experiments, they selected a version that included the most radical elements of change.

The new kitting layout was completely redesigned as was the process of selecting the parts to form the kits. The team collected data in a pilot run for two weeks. An analysis of the data revealed that

- errors had declined by more that 80 percent;
- no incomplete kits were sent to assembly;
- the people working in the area could do the job faster than before.

During this phase, the team finalized documentation for the new process and trained all personnel in the area. Control and response plans were set up to ensure this new process would not experience a slow decline with errors creeping up and causing the old problems to emerge.

One of the benefits of the new process was that everything was physically rearranged for the new kitting area. As a result, it was almost impossible for employees to revert to the old way of kitting. In other words, the new process had been "error-proofed" against the old problems because the causes of the problem had been removed or altered in ways that precluded them. With a new kitting process in place, the original goal of reducing partial shipments to customers was achieved.

Once a trial period was completed, the Six Sigma project team turned the process over to the employees in the kitting area. The next step was for the project team to visit other plant locations and show workers in those areas the methodology they had used to improve kitting.

> The black belt for this project started the project with the idea that he would learn some tools or techniques that would "fix" the shipment problem. He later said that the experience had "completely changed how he saw everything."

Conclusion

This chapter focused on the *cultural* changes that are critical to successful creation of a Lean or Six Sigma environment. Chapter 6 moves to the next level: integrating Six Sigma with Lean.

CHAPTER 6

FASTER SIX SIGMA RESULTS COME FROM A LEAN CULTURE

> One of the most noteworthy accomplishments in keeping the price of Ford products low is the gradual shortening of the production cycle. The longer an article is in the process of manufacture and the more it is moved about, the greater is its ultimate cost.
>
> HENRY FORD, 1926

The Lean movement in the United States has captured the essence of Henry Ford's statement and used it as a cornerstone for creating a Lean culture. Striving to reduce the production cycle by reducing task/cycle time, or by eliminating rework or non-value-added (NVA) steps, has become a visual and easily understood methodology for convincing the workforce to embrace Lean. From this Lean culture, many positive outcomes occur. One of the most powerful of these is faster Six Sigma results.

In recent years, many continuous improvement practitioners have jumped on the Lean/Six Sigma bandwagon, drawn there by a mantra that promises that this *blended* approach produces fast results by *doing Six Sigma projects at the speed of Lean*. In pursuit of this promising blend, some organizations have chosen to operate a Six Sigma initiative using the basic Six Sigma management structure— that is, they utilize the DMAIC model, then add in Lean's focus on waste elimination, and conduct projects from start to finish at break-neck, *kaizen*-type, speeds.

This approach may work in some cases, but it requires an intricate balance of allocating resources, time, and attention that is difficult to achieve. The number of resources required to be successful can be staggering. To conduct Six Sigma measurement and analysis at this speed properly (i.e., actually focusing on each item identified in the project charter) may require the attention of additional black belts. If this allocation of human resources is not viable, the alternative is to limit the scope and depth of the project. Additionally, the approach is often skewed: As the acquisition of accurate data becomes the primary focus, people begin ignoring Lean concepts and opportunities. This is especially true if there is a financial-threshold criteria on the amount of savings being generated by a Six Sigma project.

The best approach is *not* to blend these techniques into one effort, but to use the techniques *in an integrated manner* to derive the most benefits possible from each type of project (see Fig. 6-1). Companies entering the Six Sigma world after working with Lean have come to understand this concept. Many companies have tried both approaches, but the data show that Six Sigma projects are conducted more efficiently and effectively if Lean has already been successfully implemented.

During the past few years, many Lean companies, using Lean as their continuous improvement initiative, began to see their ROI diminish on a project-by-project basis. Companies such as Metzeler Automotive Profile Systems began looking for a way to keep their continuous improvement effort moving forward. After spending four to five years successfully implementing Lean, Metzeler's manufacturing plant managers believed that quality and process improvements with potentially large financial paybacks were still waiting to be realized. Metzeler turned to Six Sigma, not as a substitute for Lean but as a supplement that would provide accurate statistical data that could help the company locate and capitalize on additional improvement opportunities. The unexpected result of injecting Six

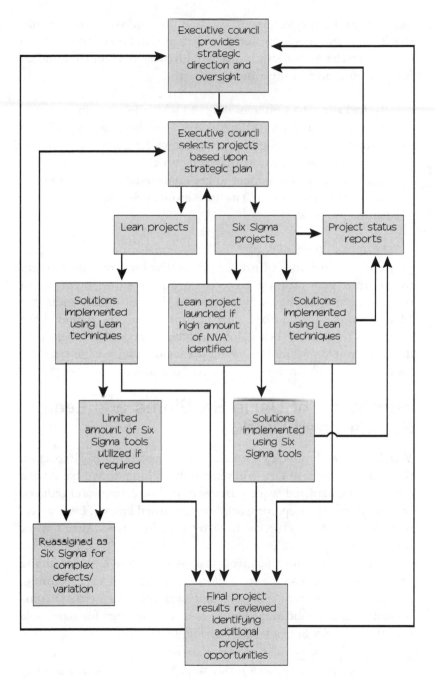

Figure 6-1.

Sigma into a Lean environment was that the company gained results much faster and much greater than anticipated. Larry Rollins, head of the Metzeler Manufacturing General Managers Council, summed up the transition and the ensuing benefits:

> We had come to a place in the road where Lean wasn't getting us the kind of ROI results we had been seeing. We needed something else to get the savings we knew were out there. Six Sigma gave us that and more. We didn't realize that our timing was perfect to get rapid results. The culture was already established. The transition to Six Sigma was a natural progression.[1]

Analyzing the results of Metzeler's initial round of Six Sigma projects—not just from a financial perspective but from the perspective of time spent on these projects—begins to show the power of using Lean and Six Sigma in tandem. In the first four months that Metzeler was utilizing Six Sigma (a time frame that included the company's initial black belt training), seven Metzeler black belts produced more than $1 million in annual savings and set the stage for more than $3 million annually in new contracts.

Benefit #1 of Using Six Sigma and Lean: Standardized Work

You do not need to look far or deep to understand Lean's impact on Six Sigma projects; in fact, you need only to look at two basic Lean concepts: standardized work (discussed in this section) and reduced number of process steps, or workflow (discussed below). Lean strives to reduce production cycle time by creating standardized work throughout a process. People do a task the same way, using best practices, every time the given task is performed. By reducing unnecessary processing, excess motion, travel, and even training, processes become even more efficient over time. As a critical component of Lean, standardized work also sets the stage for repeatable processes in a Six Sigma world (see Fig. 6-2).

---

1. From "Lean and Six Sigma: How They Work Together" presentation at the 2002 Oklahoma Manufacturing Conference, October 2002.

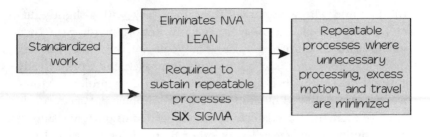

Figure 6-2.

As the Lean culture takes hold, employees accept the fact that standardized work makes their jobs simpler; they become more efficient and productive, and training new employees becomes faster and easier. This cultural shift makes it much more efficient for project teams (both Lean and Six Sigma) to see potential problems and opportunities and address them using the correct toolset at the correct time.

Six Sigma project teams working within a Lean organization can take advantage of this standardized work by identifying repeatable processes quickly through observation and related documentation, and from understanding the basic workflow of the process. Not having to spend time observing, documenting, and implementing a repeatable process can save Six Sigma project teams valuable days or even weeks in the measure, analyze, and improve phases. With standardized work already in place, the Six Sigma team can focus on opportunities quickly; there is no need to spend time determining the current state of the process and how it operates, validating the repeatability (or lack thereof), and then sorting out the routine noise from signals to identify causes of exceptional variation. The detractors of Lean often say that Lean is not scientific and allows employees to do what they want with a process without any guidelines or controls. This could not be further from the truth. The goal of creating standardized work in a Lean environment is identical to the goal of any other process improvement concept seeking to standardize work—i.e., to create simplified tasks that are done the same way every time, no matter who trains the employees performing the tasks. Unnecessary or inefficient motions and other non–value added steps are eliminated.

It does not matter whether you use Lean, or Six Sigma, or any other industrial engineering based improvement tool. The goals are still the same. The way you get there may vary, with a slightly different emphasis placed on what is truly important for your own organization or department, but the goals are the same. For Six Sigma project teams, the continuous improvement work already accomplished through Lean is a precursor to their projects. Moreover, work completed by empowered, responsible, and accountable employees provides standardized procedures that ultimately results in faster improvements regardless of other methodologies utilized.

Because all employees perform the tasks the same way each and every time, there is more opportunity for a Six Sigma team to observe and collect consistent data (see Fig. 6-3). The ensuing data analysis is more reliable because the process producing the data is already consistent and repeatable. Six Sigma can focus on reducing variation and defects, because Lean has already focused on eliminating the waste through standardized work. The end product is a synchronization of two methodologies that exceeds the individual result each is capable of producing alone. It is important to note that Lean does not necessarily have to precede Six Sigma. Some Six Sigma work may be done before Lean projects are implemented in a given area. In this situation, Lean can take advantage of any standardized work created by the Six Sigma project team.

94

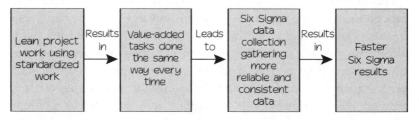

Figure 6-3.

Benefit #2 of Using Six Sigma and Lean: Reduced Process Steps

As process tasks are standardized and waste is eliminated, it is very common for the non-value-added (NVA) steps in the Lean process to be eliminated (see Fig. 6-4). This process simplification makes it much easier for the Six Sigma project team to work with a process and identify where problems and opportunities exist. Because Lean

PROCESS FLOW BEFORE AND AFTER NON-VALUE-ADDED WORK IS ELIMINATED

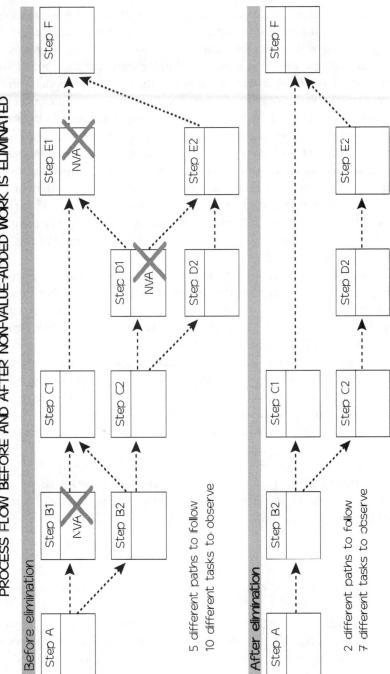

Figure 6-4.

efforts have already removed much, if not all, of the NVA steps, there are fewer paths to follow and less routine noise to distract the Six Sigma team as it probes for additional problems and opportunities.

If Lean has not been previously implemented, it is common for the Six Sigma project team to identify improvement opportunities generally viewed as "Lean" rather than "Six Sigma." Under no circumstances should these opportunities be neglected simply because they were discovered during a Six Sigma project rather than a Lean project. Instead, such opportunities should be viewed as perfect targets for synchronized Lean and Six Sigma actions, an invitation to use the tools of both methodologies to maximize the potential of the process: cleaning it up while eliminating the defects and variation. But it is prudent to understand that some of these opportunities should not signal a full-scale attack with everything available in the Six Sigma arsenal.

One of the common traps for Six Sigma project teams is getting bogged down working on low-hanging fruit with every Six Sigma tool they can pull from the toolbox. Never mind that common sense and fifteen minutes of observations can tell you that the task being watched is NVA and can be eliminated immediately without much discussion or without adverse consequences to the process or the customer. Precious days, or even weeks, can be lost dealing with these minor issues. This type of ill-advised "technical" project work can even cause project scope creep, expanding a project or forcing it to change paths because workers resist simplifying or eliminating a step.

In a Lean environment, there is less chance of this type of tactical error on the part of the Six Sigma project team to occur. Because a Lean workforce is already functioning in an environment of change, the Six Sigma project team is typically faced with one of two scenarios:

1. Most of the NVA has already been eliminated and therefore the Six Sigma team can focus on what is important without minor distractions.
2. Minor issues/opportunities are identified early in the project life cycle, NVA is identified, and root cause analysis is conducted quickly to ensure that the true cause is known. NVA is eliminated, or other minor adjustments are made quickly

because the workforce already accepts change as a part of the work environment.

This practice of reducing the number of steps in a simplified process flow directly supports the ideology of Henry Ford. By reducing the process lead time through simplification and standardization of task, the speed at which the process can operate increases while the quality and repeatability of the process improve. The end result is a better product or service at a lower cost. For the Six Sigma team, this also means a better process flow, which, in turn, makes data collection easier because there are no interruptions and operator throughput issues to deal with.

Another outcome often seen by Six Sigma teams in a Lean environment is the willingness of the workforce to cooperate with the project team. Lean organizations work extremely hard to educate the workforce on the need to change, and they provide the tools and support to help employees make change happen. As a result, employees come to expect process change as a normal part of their daily routines. As new and easier ways to work are introduced, the workforce becomes engaged in the change process. When new project teams appear in a work area, the employees expect changes to occur and are generally comfortable working with and around these change agents. This makes it much easier for the Six Sigma team to remove assignable causes (or exceptional variation) from the process without having to spend excessive amounts of time explaining and convincing the workers that this is a good thing.

97

Benefit #3 of Using Six Sigma and Lean: Accelerated Project Results

The end result of introducing Six Sigma into a Lean organization is accelerated project results. By eliminating many of the simple distractions and low-hanging fruit from the equation, it is possible to:

- address the scope and focus of a Six Sigma project much faster;
- identify issues/problems and causes without delays and interruptions;
- report out findings;
- implement solutions in a timely manner.

Although first-time Six Sigma projects in this Lean world are conducted in significantly shorter time spans than in Six Sigma organizations that have not adopted Lean, the real power comes from *the integrated and synchronized approach* using both disciplines at the correct time. Over an extended period of time, it is possible to run both Lean and Six Sigma projects in the same area; each technique complements the other, maximizing results and reducing the time span for Six Sigma projects.

The key to this approach is to recognize what issues or opportunities do not qualify as Six Sigma project targets. When a potential project does not meet Six Sigma criteria, it should not be put on the back burner or removed from the project list altogether. Instead, it should be evaluated for its potential as a good Lean project. This is not to say that every project that does not meet Six Sigma criteria should immediately become a Lean project. The determining factor is whether the executive council deems the potential project to be in alignment with the strategic goals of the organization. The council then prioritizes such projects according to their relative value in meeting the needs of the strategic plan.

The Results of a Study of Lean and Six Sigma Projects

Argent Global Services, a process engineering and management consulting firm based in Oklahoma City, analyzed a series of process improvement projects implemented in 2002 and 2003. Participating organizations were from the manufacturing and health-care sectors. The targeted projects were selected at the request of Argent clients looking for information concerning the implementation of Lean and/ or Six Sigma. The results provided great insight into the power of Lean.

Results from the Manufacturing Projects

In reviewing manufacturing projects, the study looked at thirteen Six Sigma projects in organizations where Lean was *not* practiced. The average duration of these projects was 24.1 weeks, with an average annual savings per project of $560,702.

Eleven Six Sigma projects in organizations that used Lean were also reviewed. For this group, the average project length was 17.6

98

weeks—27 percent less time than that required for the projects in organizations with no Lean initiative in place. The average annual savings per Six Sigma project in this category was $313,675—44.1 percent less than the savings for projects in organizations with no Lean initiative in place.

On the surface, it may appear that Six Sigma was less successful in Lean manufacturing organizations. However, it should be noted that the average amount of *kaizen* days applied to process improvement prior to Six Sigma project work totaled 3.8 weeks. This *kaizen* time resulted in an average annual savings of $446,181. As a result of this additional continuous improvement work, the improved results and shorter time frame demonstrates the power of synchronizing Lean and Six Sigma activities.

In addition, data collected from organizations in which Lean preceded Six Sigma showed an average project time of 21.4 weeks for all process improvement work. This total time is still 11.2 percent shorter than the time spent where Six Sigma alone was utilized. Additionally, the average total combined annual savings was $759,856—a 35.5 percent increase over the savings yielded from projects just using only Six Sigma. Figure 6-5 summarizes the manufacturing data from the study.

	# of projects	Six Sigma Avg. Time (weeks)	Six Sigma % Change	Lean Avg. Time (weeks)	Total Avg. Time (weeks)	Overall % Change	Six Sigma Avg. Annual Savings	Lean Avg. Annual Savings	Total Avg. Annual Savings
No Lean	13	24.1			24.1		$560,702		$560,702
Lean	11	17.6	27.0%	3.8	21.4	11.2%	$313,675	$446,181	$759,856

Figure 6-5. Manufacturing Projects Summary

Results from the Health-care Projects

Argent also reviewed seventeen health-care projects where no Lean was practiced. The average project length was 21.4 weeks, and the average annual savings per project was $787,167.

In the sixteen projects conducted in organizations where Lean was practiced, the average project length was only 18.1 weeks, or a decrease of 15.4 percent. The average annual savings per Six Sigma project in this group totaled $608,480, 22.7 percent less than in projects where no Lean work had been performed.

Although the results from the health-care studies were similar to the results from the manufacturing studies, there was one notable difference. Where Lean was initiated first, the dollar savings and *kaizen* event time were considerably lower. The average *kaizen* time applied prior to Six Sigma work in the health-care sector was only 1.1 weeks, with an average annual savings of $73,655. Both *kaizen* time and annual savings were significantly lower than those in the manufacturing sector. It was further determined, with few exceptions, that in the health-care organizations where Lean was utilized, the general practice was to conduct only one week of *kaizen* and then move on to another project in another area of the organization, an indication that the organizations in question did not fully understand Lean and had failed to practice continuous improvement as a part of the discipline.[2]

Even with the problems associated with this semi-implementation of Lean practices, the combined data in health care still shows very promising results. The average project time was 19.2 weeks, including *kaizen* time, which is still 10.3 percent shorter than for Six Sigma projects in a non-Lean environment. The average annual savings of the combined Lean and Six Sigma work totaled $682,135— 13.3 percent lower than for projects utilizing only Six Sigma, but this can easily be attributed to the fact that the amount of Lean effort applied was considerably less than that applied in manufacturing. Figure 6-6 summarizes the health-care results.

2. It should be noted that in the three years following this study, Lean has become a major continuous improvement methodology in health-care and that there has been an amazing increase in the number of reported Lean improvement results. In addition, Six Sigma projects in health-care facilities that have adopted Lean are being completed in record time.

	# of projects	Six Sigma Avg. Time (weeks)	Six Sigma % Change	Lean Avg. Time (weeks)	Total Avg. Time (weeks)	Overall % Change	Six Sigma Avg. Annual Savings	Lean Avg. Annual Savings	Total Avg. Annual Savings
No Lean	17	21.4			21.4		$787,167		$787,167
Lean	16	18.1	15.4%	1.1	19.2	11.2%	$608,480	$73,655	$682,135

Figure 6-6. Health-care Project Summary

Overall Results From Both Manufacturing and Health-care Projects

Combining the results of the two study groups, the data in Figure 6-7 presents a somewhat more realistic and conservative projection of the potential of synchronizing Lean and Six Sigma efforts.

	# of projects	Six Sigma Avg. Time (weeks)	Six Sigma % Change	Lean Avg. Time (weeks)	Total Avg. Time (weeks)	Overall % Change	Six Sigma Avg. Annual Savings	Lean Avg. Annual Savings	Total Avg. Annual Savings
No Lean	30	22.6			22.6		$689,032		$689,032
Lean	27	17.9	20.7%	2.2	20.1	11.0%	$488,374	$225,425	$713,799

Figure 6-7. Combined Study Summary

Using this Lean/Six Sigma synchronized approach makes it possible to blend elements of both disciplines to address all issues/opportunities within an area quickly, keep the momentum of change going, and produce significant results quickly by using the correct skill sets at the correct time. It is possible to use Lean to remove the waste and create standardized and simplified processes and then use Six Sigma to address tougher, more complex issues. Quite often, the Six Sigma team can then utilize Lean facilitators to implement changes recommended by the Six Sigma project team.

In organizations that have gone down the Lean path and then introduced Six Sigma, this synchronized back-and-forth transition between the two disciplines is seamless. Employees not only *understand* how both initiatives work together but also *expect* them to work in tandem. They don't have to know all the details and understand all the Six Sigma tools to appreciate how Lean and Six Sigma complement each other to generate significant results. Figure 6-8 summarizes the power of synchronizing Lean and Six Sigma efforts.

- Synchronization creates an environment where overall project timelines are shortened.

- Bottom-line results are increased at a more rapid pace than when either initiative is used as a stand-alone effort.

- The synchronized approach allows all employees to participate, creating faster employee buy-in.

- The approach allows black belts and champions to focus Six Sigma efforts on the more difficult issues; Lean teams can lead the way by attacking waste and "low-hanging fruit."

Figure 6-8. Benefits of Synchronizing Lean and Six Sigma Efforts

Case Study #7: Implementing Six Sigma After Successful Lean Improvement

A profitable electronics manufacturer adopted Lean manufacturing as its continuous improvement methodology after sending management team members to several Lean seminars. Facing foreign competition that was increasingly taking market share, management knew that a proactive strategy was required to retain its position in the industry.

Determined to make the cultural change necessary to support a Lean transformation, company executives drove Lean improvement from the top, requiring all employees to attend a one-day Lean introduction class.

As interest in Lean spread throughout the organization, *kaizen* events were conducted one product family at a time. As five-day *kaizen* events were completed, the executive council reviewed results with the Lean project team and outside facilitators and determined whether additional events were warranted. Events were conducted within each area until the executive council and the facilitators agreed that the value stream had been improved and that at least 80 percent of initiatives featured in the future state map had been implemented.

Metrics for each event were tied to work cell and value stream goals and objectives, which, in turn, were translated into impact statements against key performance indicators of the entire company. Success was determined by each team's performance against these metrics, regardless of total bottom-line impact. After all product family work cells had been improved through Lean techniques, the executive council reprioritized areas for future events based on the input of employees and Lean teams.

After 18 months of intense Lean improvement throughout the company's manufacturing facility, one product family stood out from all other lines and work cells. Through each reprioritization cycle, the executive council consistently ranked this product line at the top of the list for additional *kaizen*. Even though the product family had reported annual savings of more than $225,000 through four weeks of *kaizen* events, it was apparent to the executive council, the Lean facilitators, and the vast majority of the employees working in this cell that there were still several significant opportunities that the Lean teams had been unable to address successfully.

Several members of the executive council were familiar with Six Sigma and were interested in adding Six Sigma methodology to the ongoing Lean initiative. Initial reaction to this idea ranged from excited approval to cautious support to outright objection. The council members who objected to the proposal were concerned that employee enthusiasm, after eighteen months of Lean projects that involved *all* employees, would be extinguished if improvement initiatives were suddenly transferred into the hands of a select few. They feared that having Six Sigma black belts and green belts run projects, instead of using all employees to identify opportunity and implement change, would send the wrong message. Nonetheless, after extensive discussion of the pros and cons of the approach, the executive council determined that adding Six Sigma would not be detrimental to the company's culture change.

The council authorized black belt training and certification for two employees. As a part of the extensive five-week training program, each of these candidates was required to successfully complete one Six Sigma project approved by the course instructors. One of the black belt candidates was directed to focus on the work cell that continually appeared at the top of the Lean prioritization list. By selecting this particular set of opportunities as a Six Sigma project, the executive council hoped to achieve success and demonstrate a purpose for adding Six Sigma methodology to the company's Lean initiative.

The results of this first project were quite powerful and resulted in some unexpected gains. The black belt candidate assigned to this project was able to assemble a project team; create a project charter; and get his Six Sigma champion, project team, and executive council approval all within three days.

Quickly moving from the define phase to the measure and analyze phases, the project team focused on line-balancing and production rate issues. A control chart was created for fifteen months' worth of historical production rate data. Using this control chart to identify signals of possible exceptional variation, the black belt candidate noticed numerous dates on which the production rate had fallen outside of the lower control limit; he then asked line leads and the line supervisor what problems had occurred on the given dates. The supervisor had been maintaining a well-annotated production log for several years. Although this log had never been used for any specific purpose, it suddenly proved to be a very valuable source of data and clearly illustrated what had been occurring in the cell. Most of the problems uncovered were related to vendor deliveries and quality issues.

Product engineers and the production supervisor immediately began addressing vendor delivery problems and parts quality issues with several vendors. All subsequent occurrences of late deliveries were immediately reported to the purchasing department, and corrective action was initiated. At the same time, Lean visual aids were posted to help employees identify convoluted cords and defective cases.

The leads and supervisor then looked for more recent dates that problems had occurred, but they could find no other signals to review until Lean work had begun. Although there were numerous signals following the second Lean *kaizen* event, nothing that pinpointed possible problems was noted in the logs.

A decision was made to use a control chart to measure the cycle time at three distinct points on the production line and proactively address these signals as they occurred. A second chart was used to show the gap between cycle time and takt time. During the next three weeks, these control charts were used to monitor performance on the production line. At the end of this monitoring period, the team met to discuss the findings. With the exception of one late box delivery and one bad case of cords, there were no obvious answers noted on the control charts for more than a dozen signals, each occurring during a period where the leads and/or supervisor were attempting to move employees on the production line to balance the work.

Anecdotal evidence presented by one of the leads suggested that one employee, who had been identified as a roadblock by several Lean project teams, was disrupting the flow of work intentionally whenever adjustments to task content were made. Additionally, several leads expressed their belief that this employee was intentionally slowing down when the takt time was adjusted down and speeding up when the takt time was increased.

Working discreetly with only two team members (neither the line leads nor the supervisor were involved at this juncture), the black belt candidate used Design of Experiments (DOE) to measure the impact this "roadblock" had on the flow of products down the line. He observed the production process over a five-week period, both when the "roadblock" was on the line and off the line and specifically watched the worker's interaction with leads when they balanced the work and his interaction with the supervisor when she balanced the work. Data were collected and analyzed in relation to the experiment. Utilizing a *Scree Plot* to show the results graphically and comparing these results with known attendance and work assignment data, the black belt was easily able to explain what had been occurring.

The roadblock was the major cause of the signals generated. Moreover, the greatest variances were occurring when he was confronted by the supervisor in front of all employees. There was no negative impact at all when the leads balanced the assembly line by themselves, and the roadblock was not assigned a position on the line. If the supervisor intervened in this work balancing, there was a slight negative impact that was usually self-corrected by the next sampling.

Armed with this information, management removed the worker from this production line permanently. Additional soft-skills training sessions were provided for the supervisor to improve relations with the workforce. All changes implemented were quickly accepted by the workforce, and vendors became more responsive once they realized they were being monitored and penalized for quality issues.

The Six Sigma project was completed and closed after only eleven weeks of effort. The annual savings and increased production totaled nearly $155,000. The combined impact of both Lean and Six Sigma amounted to more than $335,000 annually. The workforce readily embraced the Six Sigma results and implemented the changes requested by the project team without hesitation. When questioned by the Lean facilitators about the ease of Six Sigma improvements, employees summarized the change with a simple statement:

We have come to believe in change as a way to make our work easier. Lean has taught us to try new things. What was presented by the Six Sigma team made sense. We did not understand all of the Six Sigma techniques utilized, but the project team explained enough that we understood that the results would be good. So, why not try it? After all, if it doesn't work, we can always try something else.

The culture was right. The low-hanging fruit had been removed. Lean improvements had enabled a black belt candidate to show swift and effective results when applying Six Sigma solutions after Lean had made several passes at the value stream.

Case Study #8: Faster Six Sigma Results to Produce Complex Electrical Circuits

A manufacturer of complex electrical circuits was having difficulty with defects in the final product and with meeting the schedule required by the customer. To correct the defects, the product was dismantled and rebuilt. The current first pass yield was in the mid-40 percent range and the company was not shipping the requested number of units each week. Several attempts to improve the situation had been initiated, but none of these was successful. When the manufacturer decided to launch a Six Sigma initiative, one of the first projects to be addressed was the improvement of the process for this complex electrical circuit.

During the define phase, the black belt and champion set up the project charter for the team. The goal was to eliminate the defects in the circuit and improve first pass yield so the company could meet the shipping schedule. During this phase, the team also identified the critical-to-quality (CTQ) characteristics from the customer and translated these CTQs to specific measures of the product.

The measure phase focused on setting up data collection plans for the CTQs and several of the process measures. Data already collected for several of the measures could be analyzed immediately. The team also made a process map to track the production of the circuit from the initial kitting of the components to the final inspection of the completed unit. During the construction of the process map, the team would actually follow the process physically to make sure the process map reflected the current state. After the initial "walk through" of the process, the team members realized that there were a number of changes that needed to be implemented immediately. These included

- cleaning the assembly area and setting up a cleaning schedule;
- using the standard operating procedures (SOPs) consistently;
- documenting the flow of each unit through assembly.

Much of the activity that took place during the measure phase would already have been completed had the manufacturer engaged in a Lean implementation prior to the Six Sigma initiative. Lean tools, such as 5S, focus on the order and organization in an area; using these tools first would have saved time for the Six Sigma project.

Because the defect associated with the low first-pass yield could not be seen until the unit was assembled, the analyze phase focused mainly on the final CTQs. Using process behavior charts on various details, the team was able to pinpoint specific weak spots in the circuit. These were traced back to specific steps in the process. At each specific step, the team identified factors that might cause the defect.

In the improve phase, the team set up experiments to determine which factors (with several possible versions of each factor) had the greatest impact on the defect. The results of several experiments led to process changes that the team implemented. A pilot study of these changes indicated that the first pass yield was near 90 percent, a significant improvement over the original mid-40 percent first pass yield at the start of the project.

The control phase focused on writing new standard operating procedures, training the operators in the new process, and setting up process behavior charts for ongoing monitoring of the process. Response plans were put in place to find and eliminate exceptional causes of variation when they occurred.

After one month of trials, the project team turned the process over to the process owners for continuing operation.

This Six Sigma project took about eight months to complete. If the activities associated with Lean had already been completed, the time for this project would have been shorter. In addition, the black belt and project team were working on a part-time basis. Projects that are under the leadership of a full-time black belt can be completed in a shorter time.

Conclusion

This chapter—and the accompanying case studies—describes and illustrates the benefits of implementing Six Sigma in a Lean culture. Chapter 7 shows how to select and apply the right methodology to maximize your success.

LEAN OR SIX SIGMA: APPLYING THE RIGHT METHODOLOGY

It is important that an aim never be defined in terms of activity or methods. It must always relate directly to how life is better for everyone....The aim of the system must be clear to everyone in the system. The aim must include plans for the future. The aim is a value judgment.

DR. W. EDWARDS DEMING

When seeking a continuous improvement (CI) project to work on, it is not enough to merely identify a problem with an opportunity for improvement. The project you select must be selected based on some criteria and must be directly related to the strategic goals of the organization. All too often, companies initiate a continuous improvement effort with little or no strategic planning; in doing so, they also fail to provide a vision or goals. When this occurs, the CI initiative—regardless of the methodology utilized—will tend to wander aimlessly until it dies from lack of results, cohesiveness, or support from the workforce. For any CI initiative to be truly successful, you must set your sights on a common goal and stay focused on that goal.

Having strategic goals in place makes it possible to maintain the effort continuously; it also facilitates using more than one CI discipline to achieve the purpose, either simultaneously or sequentially.

Using Lean and Six Sigma in an integrated approach requires a synchronization that endures throughout the process. All potential projects must be reviewed and analyzed to determine

- which discipline will work best;
- in what order to use one technique or the other;
- when to change from one methodology to the other.

The structure and management of this synchronized approach must be very clear to everyone throughout the organization. It is equally important for everyone to understand that a successful CI culture does not simply change for the sake of change; all proposed change initiatives must result in improved efficiency and lower cost. At the same time they must conform to and reflect the goals and direction of the organization. Once these connections are clear to employees, they begin to accept change. It is at this point that the process acquires a momentum of its own—results come at a faster pace, because the organization has accepted a culture of change as a standard condition.

Choose the Right Projects

Once the stage has been set for change (and this always includes employee buy-in), it is critical to choose the right project. The idea behind choosing the right project is to pick a project that meets the following criteria:

- It aligns with the strategic goals of the organization.
- Project goals and objectives can be clearly communicated to the workforce in the project area.
- There is a high probability of success (at least during the early stages of Lean and/or Six Sigma work) that has the power to convince the workforce of the validity and power of CI initiatives.

All selected projects must focus on the strategic goals of the organization and must be defined by objectives that move the organization closer to those goals. The project goals and objectives must be clearly communicated to employees, who must also understand how a successful project will assist the company move toward the future state set out in the organization's strategic goals. In providing this information, management also provides a clear sense of mission for each project (see Fig. 7-1).

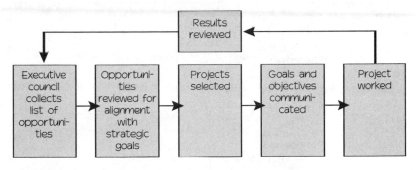

Figure 7-1.

This broad framework provides parameters for project selection, but how do you actually choose the right project? For a synchronized Lean Six Sigma approach, the path to success can be found within the methodologies of both disciplines. For organizations that have already begun a Lean journey, it is fairly easy to roll the Lean project selection process into Six Sigma. Management begins the process of identifying the "right" project by reviewing potential projects, analyzing the expected results, and seeing if and how they align with the strategic goals of the company. This knowledge can then be combined with ancillary objectives used in Lean project selection.

In choosing an initial project, some companies opt for an easy success that will demonstrate a Lean or Six Sigma technique; others focus on a project that will deliver the greatest ROI or will address or resolve the most challenging problem/opportunity. In some cases, management will choose to work with the group of employees most receptive to change.

A typical project selection strategy in a Lean environment is to prioritize the value stream. As companies move to integrate Six Sigma into a Lean environment, staying with this strategy of prioritization can keep the overall structure synchronized and simplistic. For companies that choose a Six Sigma project selection process, the path is somewhat different. In either case, the projects considered must meet certain basic criteria (see Fig. 7-2).

SELECTION PATHS FOR SUCCESSFUL PROJECTS

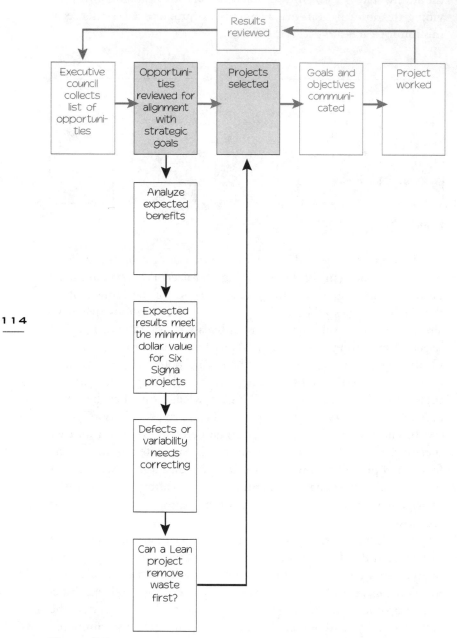

114

Figure 7-2.

If you think a potential project might make a good Six Sigma project, consider the following questions:

- Does it align with the strategic goals of the organization?
- Does the dollar estimate meet the minimum amount of expected cost savings at project completion to qualify as a Six Sigma project?
- Do defects or variability that need correcting exist?

Lean projects must meet Lean criteria. For example:

- Has waste been identified?
- Is there an opportunity to simplify processes or shorten process lead time (a sure sign that there is waste in the process)?
- Is the potential project top priority after a value stream mapping exercise has developed an action plan for improvement?

Regardless of the approach, the project selected must be directly tied to the value chain and associated support processes of the organization. The "value chain" of your organization is the heart of your company: It is the product or service that your organization produces or performs and that your customer buys. Every project chosen should focus on improving the value chain or the functions that support it.

To facilitate project selection, you must determine which processes need to be optimized and in what order. Processes chosen for Six Sigma improvement require baseline data that can validate potential opportunities before projects are chosen, whereas processes selected for Lean projects should have measurable goals and objectives that can be related to the strategic goals of the organization. Six Sigma opportunities must be evaluated to ensure that only high-priority issues that meet Six Sigma criteria are initiated as Six Sigma projects. Lean opportunities, however, are often chosen with little regard to overall strategic priority if the goal is to assist the organization in creating a culture of change.

As you work to identify potential projects, you also need to look at areas of opportunity. Ask the following questions:

1. What is the single biggest threat to our business/organization today?
2. What is the single biggest opportunity we have today?

3. Where are we not meeting critical customer standards? And what data are available to support this effort?
4. Where are we not meeting critical performance standards? And what data are available to support this effort?
5. If I/we had a "magic wand" and could instantly change one thing in the organization, what would it be?
6. What changes are anticipated that could create threats or opportunities for our business?

Once you have used these questions to evaluate your list of potential projects, you need to review the potential impact of each of the projects on the organization and its strategic goals. The executive council should review how *meaningful* a project might be in relation to business and operational performance, customer satisfaction, or organizational performance. Additionally, the project should be reviewed for organizational and *technical feasibility* (i.e., is it manageable?).

If this Six Sigma project-selection approach disqualifies a potential project from consideration, return to your organization's Lean project-selection strategy and see if the project meets the criteria from this direction. Identifying waste in the process and understanding customer expectations can you help determine project potential, regardless of the organization's Lean project strategy.

Choose the Right Approach

Hand in hand with choosing the right project is choosing the right approach. It does no good to choose a very simple "low-hanging fruit" problem/opportunity for a project and then use Six Sigma methodology to laboriously validate the issues and create solutions over the course of several months. Nor does it serve any purpose to select an extremely severe defect, repeatability, or variation problem and attempt to find the root cause, validate it, and determine the perfect state using only Lean tools. Attempting to correct extremely difficult issues with the quick-hitting, waste-focused methodology of Lean rarely works for problems with root causes that are buried under a mound of detailed knowledge that no one can fathom.

The secret to success is to have the executive council analyze the project selected and determine the best approach. This is generally a simple task. More than likely, the project will initially be reviewed by the executive council in cooperation with both Lean masters and Six Sigma black belts. During this review, many things will be obvious and will require no protracted discussions or analyses. A review, for example, may immediately reveal "low-hanging fruit" and there will be little to discuss because everyone understands that a Lean approach is the obvious choice. Lean can quickly provide financially significant results and Lean changes that have a real impact on the workforce can be quickly implemented. Often, however, this type of project also reveals defects, repeatability, and/or variability, issues that Lean technique cannot adequately solve. This presents a perfect opportunity to change gears and use Six Sigma as the methodology for an additional project.

At other times, a project selected by the executive council may already focus on a complex issue that demands an analysis of very detailed information and can only be described in very specific numerical terms. With projects of this type, it will probably be necessary to review past efforts at correcting the problem. The overall review may include a discussion on estimated savings that should occur after the problem has been corrected. For projects with these characteristics, the obvious methodology is Six Sigma (see Fig. 7-3).

Clearly, not all projects will be this straightforward. For most projects, selecting the appropriate approach will require a review of the project-selection criteria to ensure that minimum requirements for one methodology or the other are met (see Fig. 7-4). Typically, the executive council begins this process by comparing the project against Six Sigma criteria. If the project does not measure up to, it can then be evaluated to see if it is a viable Lean project. If it is, the project can then be assigned to a Lean team and set in motion.

Deciding which approach should be utilized may also be influenced by the workforce. In very structured, traditional culture organizations that have relied heavily on Six Sigma or other statistically based improvement techniques, the workforce may be resistant to using Lean. In such cases, even if the executive council believes the project to be classified as "low-hanging fruit," it may be more beneficial to use Six Sigma. This avoids arguments wrapped around the validity of results; it can also create opportunities. Because the Six Sigma approach is designed to probe beyond low-hanging fruit,

SIMPLE LEAN OR SIX SIGMA APPROACH DECISIONS

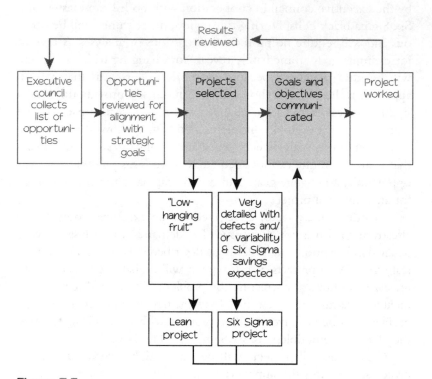

Figure 7-3.

the project team may find associated quality or variability issues. This approach may also work in organizations that embrace the concepts of Lean, if organizational history supports the theory that low-hanging fruit sometimes masks defect and variability problems that require hard data.

Organizations accustomed to Lean continuous improvement efforts may also struggle with matching a project with an appropriate methodology. Many of these organizations find that it is easier to attack projects with Lean, even those projects that are a perfect fit for Six Sigma. The advantage to this is that Lean improvement will clean up low-hanging fruit quickly and can then serve as a springboard for transitioning to Six Sigma, which tackles the more difficult issues that remain. Because the culture is already rooted in the

COMPLEX LEAN OR SIX SIGMA APPROACH DECISIONS

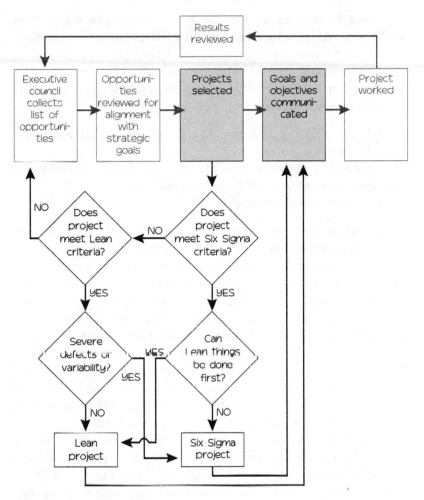

Figure 7-4.

119

concept of never-ending change in every aspect of the organization, the workforce is not leery of methodology changes. Because of this, the transition to Six Sigma is not likely to meet with much resistance, particularly if management has clearly communicated to employees the benefits of using both methodologies to foster continuous improvement.

Choose the Right People

Choosing the right people for your project team is just as important as choosing the right approach. Team members can quickly implode a project for a variety of reasons, and one poor choice when selecting a project team may fatally doom the project before it ever gets off the ground. How effective will your team be, for example, if even one member of the team

- lacks credibility with other team members or with employees in the project area?
- exhibits personality traits that are completely "out of sync" with the other members of the team?
- has a "controlling" ego?

It is important to point out that people with these characteristics will have a different impact on Lean projects than on Six Sigma projects because of the underlying structures of the two methodologies. For example, because Lean environments encourage global participation of the workforce, the controlling ego problem is more likely to surface in Lean projects than in Six Sigma projects. Many engineers, supervisors, and managers place themselves at odds with the workforce without knowing it. As subject matter experts (SMEs), these management and professional staff members can elevate themselves (quite often unintentionally) above the workforce because of their process or product knowledge. Over time, workers tend to resent this social "caste" system and the SME.

Staff members who have already earned this reputation among workers in a given area should not be assigned to project teams in that area. Instead, they should be reassigned to projects outside of their primary area of influence and knowledge. Lean methodology relies heavily on team-based decision making; to take full advantage of this team-based concept, it is better to avoid project team members that cannot function well within this egalitarian framework.

Lean projects do, however, benefit greatly from strong SMEs who have small or subdued egos and do not have to be in charge. Teaming this type of personality with other natural leaders from all ranks of the organization helps ensure that the Lean team approach is successful. True Lean leaders cooperate; they do not compete with one another for supremacy on a team but work together to divide and conquer project tasks swiftly, without hesitation, and without "attitude."

The SMEs on your Lean project teams must have more than the correct attitude. They must have the appropriate knowledge for the project they will be working on, and this means your team will include a pretty eclectic group of individuals: process knowledge (i.e., frontline workers), product or service knowledge (i.e., product engineers or similar professionals), equipment knowledge (i.e., maintenance technicians), facility knowledge, etc.

$$\begin{array}{c}\text{Lean} \\ \text{facilitator}\end{array} + \begin{array}{c}\text{Subject} \\ \text{matter} \\ \text{experts}\end{array} + \begin{array}{c}\text{Natural} \\ \text{leaders} \\ \text{from the} \\ \text{workforce}\end{array} - \begin{array}{c}\text{Controlling} \\ \text{egos}\end{array} = \begin{array}{c}\text{Successful} \\ \text{project} \\ \text{team}\end{array}$$

Figure 7-5. Selecting a Successful Lean Project Team

Six Sigma projects also depend on SMEs, but their full-time participation on a core project team is not as critical. If you assign full-time black and green belts who have a good general knowledge of the process, product and/or service to the team, you can then bring in SMEs that have specific knowledge as needed and when needed. This approach is practical and possible because the power of a Six Sigma project lies in the *numbers*. If the data are analyzed and reported in a clear and concise manner, it is much easier to get the desired results because many of the implementation decisions can be made by the black belt and the champion, not by majority vote as in the case of many Lean projects.

Six Sigma projects must be staffed by credible black belts and green belts who are well respected within the organization. Their broad knowledge is supplemented by SMEs with specific knowledge of the project area or other relevant knowledge. In many instances, Six Sigma black belts are chosen for their leadership potential, but on ideal project teams, they are also paired with natural leaders from the workforce of the target area. Figure 7-6 illustrates the basic equation of the ideal Six Sigma project team. However, some organizations have made the fatal mistake of sending some candidates to black or green belt training "just to get them out of our hair." This upfront attitude almost always ensures that any project these belts are assigned to will experience pushback or other roadblocks from the workforce. Selecting the right people for your project team, regardless of the approach used, is important.

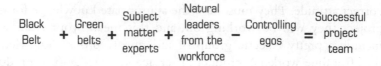

Figure 7-6. Selecting a Successful Six Sigma Project Team

Choose the Right Tools

The final piece of the project-selection puzzle is tool selection. Both Lean and Six Sigma are multitool approaches. Each requires knowledge of how and when to use a given tool.

Black belts and green belts working on Six Sigma projects must select the correct tools to address specific problems. If the belts have not been properly educated or do not have enough experience, the results can be disastrous. Inadequate tool knowledge, for example, can lead to long, drawn-out projects with project teams using every Six Sigma available, simply because the tools exist. Misguided belts may create a host of improperly used control charts, which measure the wrong things at the wrong intervals, or histograms that provide an analysis of data that has no relationship to the current project.

Many Lean projects suffer from the "cookie-cutter" approach to tool selection. If a tool or toolset was successfully used on one project, the project team may decide to use it on the next project (or every project), simply because it worked well before. As each new project is completed, however, it becomes obvious that the results are not nearly as strong as they were when the initial project was completed. Regardless of the approach selected, it is imperative to choose tools that are appropriate for the assigned project. Six Sigma belts and Lean facilitators must have a basic knowledge of which tools are available and which tools are the best tools for accomplishing any given task. Selecting the right tool at the right time ensures that each phase of the project will proceed much more efficiently and effectively; results will be stronger, and the workforce will be more willing to accept implemented changes. The power of Lean resides in its ability to remove waste quickly and methodically from the process. But this is accomplished by using the right tools. If the wrong tool is used, the consequences can range from delays to breakdowns. Six Sigma projects handled properly with the correct tools can produce very powerful results. If the Six Sigma project follows Lean, and if the project results have a positive impact on a process, frontline employees with limited statistical or analytical knowledge will be more receptive to Six Sigma. If the results are questionable, the same employees will not have much faith in the new methodology. For this reason alone, belts need to ensure that they do not stumble with their Six Sigma tools. Like their Lean counterparts, they must select the right tools for the right tasks.

Where Lean and Six Sigma are integrated, using proper tools can yield exceptionally good results. Lean tools can often provide the implementation strategy for making changes after the Six Sigma work has identified causes and preferred solutions. Moreover, many Six Sigma Black Belts have discovered that Lean tools provide a flexible and effective implementation path for their Six Sigma solutions. Because Lean tools are readily accepted by the workforce, implementation of Six Sigma changes becomes much easier for the project team.

123

Conclusion

This chapter described how to choose the right projects, the right approach, the right people, and the right tools when implementing Lean, Six Sigma, or some combination of both. Chapter 8 shows how to maximize the potential of Lean and Six Sigma by *synchronizing* the two initiatives.

THE TWO-PRONGED APPROACH: SYNCHRONIZING LEAN AND SIX SIGMA

> I still get questions about how Lean compares with Six Sigma, Total Productive Maintenance, Business Process Re-engineering, Demand-Flow, the Theory of Constraints, and other approaches to improvement. And I always give the same answer: At the end of the day, we are all trying to achieve the same thing: The perfect value stream.
>
> JAMES WOMACK

If, as James Womack asserts, the goal of all continuous improvement methodologies truly is the same—i.e., trying to perfect the value stream—it only makes sense that you should use Lean and Six Sigma together, along with any other continuous improvement initiative that can help you achieve perfection. The problem lies in *how* you use various initiatives at the same time. Lean and Six Sigma used in a *synchronized approach* provide strong results and move you closer to that "perfect" value stream much faster than using only one approach at a time, or worse yet, using a hodge-podge of techniques that work against one another.

Use Lean and Six Sigma to Attain Strategic Goals

As organizations learn to synchronize their Lean and Six Sigma initiatives, they also learn that Lean and Six Sigma rely on each other. Many continuous improvement initiatives have been launched as stand-alone efforts aimed at improving processes and quality. Even in the recent past, using a single initiative as the entire CI focus for an entire organization has been fairly common practice. But it has become increasingly apparent that no single initiative can address everything required to move a process or organization as close to perfection as possible.

As companies like Metzeler Automotive Profile Systems have discovered (refer back to chapter 6), at a given point in time, an organization must introduce other CI disciplines to deal with the issues and opportunities that the CI initiative already in place does not adequately address. With Lean, as waste is driven from a value stream, the voice of the customer becomes louder and louder (see Fig. 8-1). Focus shifts from driving out waste to ensuring that customer demands and expectations are met. As these expectations present themselves, it is not always possible to use the basic Lean toolbox to resolve the issues that emerge with them. Other CI tools are better equipped to address these new opportunities.

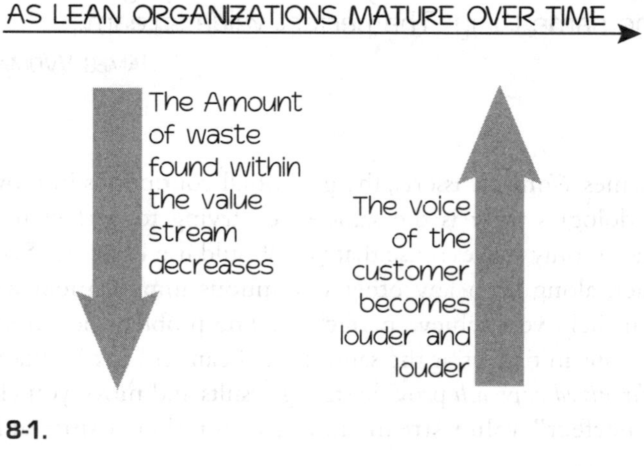

126

AS LEAN ORGANIZATIONS MATURE OVER TIME

The Amount of waste found within the value stream decreases

The voice of the customer becomes louder and louder

Figure 8-1.

Lean's reliance on Six Sigma is rooted in Lean's greatest strength, which is paradoxically Lean's greatest limitation. Lean is a very fast-moving methodology that attacks waste. It relies on the knowledge and skills of the workforce not only to assist in identifying opportunities but also in implementing solutions. The mathematical and statistical tools used in Lean are basic and designed to support this fast-based approach to waste elimination. By its very nature, Lean does not have within its basic toolset a way to address complex defect and repeatability issues (see Fig. 8-2). As Lean organizations mature, project results begin to get smaller in direct proportion to the number of projects completed over an extended period of time. Thus, these organizations must begin to look for other CI tools to move them forward in their CI journey. Many of these organizations have discovered the power of Six Sigma to propel this forward motion.

OPPORTUNITIES FOR IMPROVEMENT

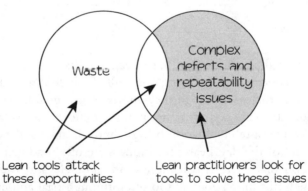

Figure 8-2.

At the same time, Six Sigma practitioners have come to learn that Lean provides a powerful addition to the Six Sigma toolset. In organizations that use Six Sigma as a CI initiative, many CI opportunities are overlooked or positioned low on priority lists because the projected dollar value of projects that might effectively deal with these opportunities does not measure up to Six Sigma criteria. But using this financial factor as the sole determinant is impractical, because the issues targeted by the proposed projects should not be ignored or overlooked. Quite often, projects that do not meet the financial impact requirements of Six Sigma can become Lean projects. Moreover, as Lean quickly resolves the targeted issues, it frequently provides insights that suggest more promising Six Sigma projects.

Additionally, many Six Sigma organizations have come to recognize the power of Lean implementation concepts when changing processes. After identifying the issues, these organizations use Lean tools, techniques, and people to implement solutions that will facilitate future Six Sigma initiatives (see Fig. 8-3). This integration of the two disciplines creates a powerful CI strategy that embraces the statistical structure of Six Sigma, the speed of Lean, and the participation of the workforce in the actual change process.

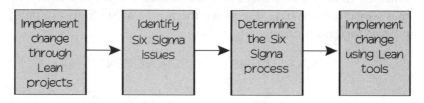

Figure 8-3.

In a nutshell, the goal of both Lean and Six Sigma is to reduce cost and reduce defects and variation—all of which can be defined as waste in a process. Although they approach this goal from different directions, they are complementary in their efforts. Lean's fast-paced approach to waste elimination brings almost immediate results. Yet, at the end of the day, Lean practitioners are often saddled with the realization that there is still money on the table and issues to be addressed. But they know, all too often through trial and error, that Lean technique alone cannot handle these opportunities effectively. Six Sigma can and will. Where Lean slows down, Six Sigma can pick up the pace, address the issues, and keep the initiative moving. Moreover, the progression from Lean to Six Sigma is very natural.

What practitioners of both Lean and Six Sigma must realize, however, is that integrating the two methodologies does not mean taking one initiative or the other as far as you can go and then switching to the next toolset. And it most assuredly is not about creating a combined initiative that runs Six Sigma projects at lightning speed or Lean projects without workforce involvement. The two-pronged approach to success relies on using Lean and Six Sigma in a synchronized manner, capturing ongoing results by taking advantage of *the appropriate approach at the appropriate time.* As organizations explore the potential of using both Lean and Six Sigma during the CI journey, another fact that soon becomes apparent is that this two-pronged approach yields results that are even more impressive if the two disciplines are *synchronized early* in the overall CI initiative.

A single executive council focused on the strategic goals of the organization is the primary meeting point for these two CI initiatives (see Fig. 8-4). This is a matter of logistics. To coordinate continuous and parallel improvement efforts, there must be a single entity (namely the executive council) in charge of project prioriti-

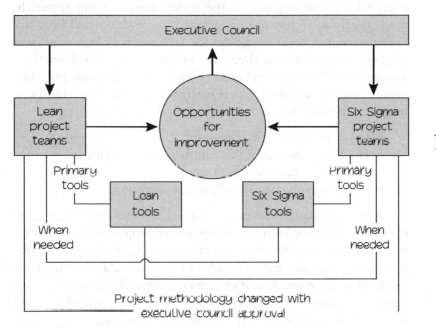

Figure 8-4.

zation, coordination, and the review of results on the strategic goals of the organization. This council must recognize the individual value of Lean and Six Sigma. Additionally, the council must understand the power of Lean teams using appropriate Six Sigma tools and Six Sigma teams using Lean tools. An executive council charged with successful completion of the CI initiative must also teach CI teams the secret of using appropriate tools and techniques at the appropriate times.

Synchronize the Two Initiatives to Maximize Results

The executive council should use a two-pronged approach to project prioritization and selection. By starting with the criteria for Six Sigma, and by eliminating all possibilities that do not meet the organization's Six Sigma criteria, the council sets the stage for success. The council must prioritize the possible Six Sigma projects based on their relationship to the strategic goals of the organization and their potential financial impact. For the second prong of this approach, the council can review the projects that were eliminated from Six Sigma consideration as candidates for Lean methodology. Any Lean projects selected should then also be prioritized based on their alignment with the strategic goals of the organization and any additional Lean prioritization criteria set by the council. These Lean criteria may include, but are not limited to, the following:

• The fastest return on investment
• The ability to change the culture of the workforce
• The fastest implementation time
• The greatest perceived pain to the workforce

As the CI initiative moves forward and as results are evaluated, the council must review both lists of prioritized projects and reprioritize as necessary to keep the momentum flowing and to keep the initiative aligned with the strategic goals of the organization. Throughout the journey, the council must encourage Lean and Six Sigma project teams to communicate with each other about needs, roadblocks, and results within working projects. Because the council is charged with keeping the overall CI initiative on course and in alignment with the strategic goals of the company, its periodic review of both Lean and Six Sigma efforts is necessary to keep the focus crisp. This council's approach to synchronization is summarized in Figure 8-5.

Having Lean and Six Sigma project teams operate totally independent of each other, especially if each team uses only its own toolset, defeats the purpose and is obviously wasteful. On the other hand, you cannot allow a project team using one methodology to

---

1. Identify opportunities, issues, and pain points.

2. Review each project opportunity against Six Sigma criteria to create a Six Sigma "potential project" list.

3. Eliminate all opportunities that do not meet Six Sigma criteria.

4. Prioritize Six Sigma potential project list.

5. Review "eliminated" Six Sigma opportunities for potential Lean projects.

6. Prioritize Lean selections.

7. Initiate both Lean and Six Sigma projects.

Figure 8-5. Project Prioritization & Selection using Six Sigma and Lean

turn over a project to a team using the other methodology without risking project creep. Doing so can lead to additional waste in the form of unnecessary or excess processing if vital information gathered by the first team is ignored by the second team.

The solution is to train all CI team members, regardless of their primary methodology, to use certain tools from either methodology. If team members know which toolset to use when and are comfortable with an interactive use of tools, projects can move forward without interruption, even when a project team sees the need for the other methodology to address an immediate concern or opportunity (see Fig. 8.6).

It makes perfect sense to equip all CI project managers, facilitators, and belts with a common understanding of both methodologies and selected skills from each. If additional tools are needed, subject matter experts (SMEs) can step in. If help from an SME is required, the project should be reviewed to consider the following:

- Can the additional tools be utilized without experiencing project creep?
- Will the project remain aligned with the strategic goals of the organization?

If the answer to either of these questions is "no," the correct course of action is to move to closure and end the project. Place the newly identified issue before the executive council for review, and let the council determine whether the opportunity meets the criteria for either CI path.

131

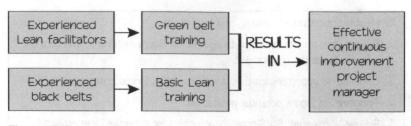

Figure 8-6.

The discussion above has focused primarily on synchronization, prioritization, alignment with strategic goals, and the functions of the executive council to ensure that Lean, Six Sigma, project teams, and the workforce are well served by the integrative process. It would be remiss not to include in this discussion a brief overview of the tools used by each discipline for cross-disciplinary purposes.

The most common Six Sigma tool used by Lean teams is the control chart (or as previously called, a process behavior chart). This very basic Six Sigma tool is at the heart of all Six Sigma projects, and it can provide a great deal of useful information and many insights to a Lean team during a single *kaizen* event (Lean project). It typically utilizes data collected by the team during the event. At times, a control chart will also include relevant historical data.

Using the signals highlighted on a control chart, a Lean team can quickly identify opportunities to address during an event. Numerous computer software products can greatly simplify the creation of control charts. Equipping Lean teams with this type of software and teaching them what and when to measure, as well as how to interpret the data on the charts, can accelerate the speed at which Lean improvements can be made.

Likewise, Six Sigma projects can benefit greatly from the use of Lean tools. Training Six Sigma Belts to identify "the eight wastes of Lean" is just the start (refer back to chapter 2 for a review of the eight wastes). In conjunction with this training, belts should be trained to use the following basic Lean tools.

Value Stream Mapping (VSM)

Organizations can greatly enhance the ability to explain to the workforce the goals and objectives of a Six Sigma project through the use of VSM. Process mapping using the VSM technique makes it much easier for a project team to explain process problems and opportunities to a group of workers, because this type of mapping creates a picture (or snapshot) of what the process (i.e., the value stream) looks like at a given point in time. This picture flows right to left, with the physical process flow on the bottom and communication on the top of the map. Employees can generally grasp the concepts portrayed through a map in 15 to 30 minutes, and this gives VSM a decisive advantage over traditional flowcharts, which are often confusing.

Five S

Belts trained to use Five S (5S) can often clean up and organize a project area quickly (see Fig. 8-7). This cleaning and organization can reduce variability in a process and also reduce the amount of "noise" within the process, which is displayed on the process control chart.

CONTROL CHART FOR CELL #5

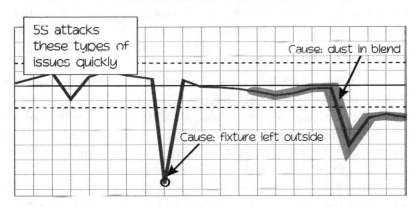

Figure 8-7.

Finding a place for everything that belongs in an area and eliminating anything that does not, reduces the amount of time it takes for a process to cycle through each occurrence. Adding visual controls that help regulate the work performed can create a more stable process without over-analysis.

Standardized Work

Creating standardized work with Lean methodology will also accelerate the speed of a Six Sigma project because, once again, this can reduce process variability and provide the workforce with basic instructions to repeat the expected process steps time and time again. This concept of repeatability is not only imperative for the success of the Six Sigma project but is also key to achieving the following goals:

- Creating a process that employees can learn quickly
- Improving throughput without increasing the speed of their work
- Providing a single methodology for tasks that need to be passed on through training to other (often new) employees

Layout and Process Flow

Teaching Six Sigma belts the Lean concepts of layout and process flow can simplify many tasks performed by Six Sigma teams. By rearranging the layout of an area so that the process actually flows from task to task with as little travel distance as possible, allows the project team to see the process in step order. The new layout also exposes process flaws, which may have been hidden with the "old" layout by travel and/or waiting.

The key to Six Sigma teams using these Lean tools is to have them move swiftly once Lean opportunities present themselves (see Fig. 8-8). Lean implementation means avoiding undue analysis of a situation. The objective here is to make a decision, make change happen, and if it isn't right, change it back or change it again. Use the results to "see" the process and improve the process.

As the layers of opportunity are peeled back, the team can start addressing the tougher issues that established the project as a Six Sigma project in the first place. If a Six Sigma team has a problem moving quickly, it is in the best interest of the organization to add a skilled Lean practitioner to its Six Sigma teams. The role of this Lean member is not to impose Lean methodology on the project by force but to bring Lean tools to the table at the opportune moment.

It is important to integrate Lean and Six Sigma tools at the appropriate time. It is also important to return projects, which may or may

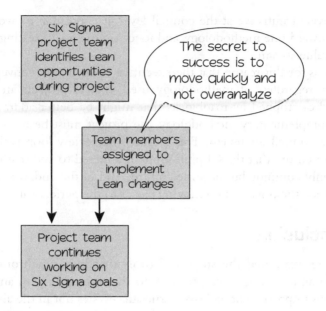

Figure 8-8.

not be completed, to the executive council to review for additional project work using the complementary toolset that can and will maximize the results obtained by the organization. This approach enables project teams to move quickly when an opportunity presents itself and shows that Lean is a viable and desirable approach for CI. In-depth analysis and determination of defect or variability through the use of Six Sigma can be used when quality standards and customer expectations require a more cautious and analytical approach.

Knowing when to shift gears and making this knowledge part of the culture is the difficult part. It is difficult because Lean "experts" will tend to try to solve all problems and issues with Lean tools, and Six Sigma belts will attempt to rely solely on Six Sigma tools. If the organization attempts to blend the initiative below the executive council level, one methodology or the other may become dominant. Assigning a single manager or department to run both initiatives will almost certainly result in either Lean or Six Sigma being placed in a secondary role. But by *synchronizing* the use of both tool sets within the organization and controlling the overall initiative at the council level, it is possible to avoid this bias toward one methodology, and focus on the goal: creating a perfect value stream.

It is for this reason that the executive council *must* convey to all teams, regardless of methodology used, that as projects are completed or stopped by roadblocks that might be better addressed by the complementary methodology, the project must be resubmitted to the council for review. This closure and review loop is the best way to ensure that the CI philosophy is adhered to and that CI will not only continue but become culture. And in the end, this is what will keep the organization moving closer to the perfect value stream.

Conclusion

Having examined the steps and tools that best synchronize Six Sigma and Lean, it is time to look to the future. As with any continuous improvement endeavor, true success lies not in the ability to improve a process or a system once, but in the ability to sustain the improvement and build upon it through ongoing initiatives. The concluding chapter of this work explores how this works best in an environment that is receptive to and comfortable with continuous improvement.

CHAPTER 9

BEYOND LEAN AND SIX SIGMA: FROM PROJECT FOCUS TO FUTURE FOCUS

For want of a nail, the shoe was lost,
For want of a shoe, the horse was lost,
For want of a horse, the rider was lost,
For want of a rider, the battle was lost,
For want of a battle, the kingdom was lost, and
All for the want of a horseshoe nail.

MOTHER GOOSE

The historical focus of improvement projects has always been on successful project completion. Once goals of the individual project are achieved, the incremental results are measured and reported, and it is laid to rest. Then the next project is initiated. In recent years, this approach to process improvement has been losing ground as more and more organizations are exploring the advantages of shifting the focus from project to continuous improvement. At the forefront of this shift are Lean and Strategy-driven Six Sigma.™

At one time, project managers ignored obvious opportunities that were not within the scope of their project even if those opportunities had the potential to improve the anticipated results. In contrast, today's continuous improvement teams recognize that every problem, issue, and/or opportunity—no matter how small—can be the basis for positive change that can have an impact on the process. It is this changing perspective that has brought Lean and Six Sigma together. Once considered competing methodologies, the two disciplines have now become compatible partners in the continuous improvement enterprise. Furthermore, organizations that have adopted a synchronized approach to Lean and Six Sigma are experiencing a cultural shift within their workforces. The basic tenets of Lean rely on the workforce to identify and eliminate waste throughout the value stream. Part of this approach includes addressing as much opportunity as possible within the framework of a *kaizen* event. Including the workforce in the change process is a critical piece of the strategy to change the culture so that workers not only accept change but embrace it. By utilizing the workforce to find opportunities for improvement, CI teams have the ability to move the continuous improvement initiative forward in an environment receptive to change (see Fig. 9-1).

138

CREATING AN ENVIRONMENT RECEPTIVE TO CHANGE

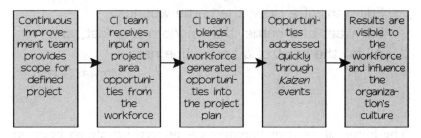

| Continuous Improvement team provides scope for defined project | → | CI team receives input on project area opportunities from the workforce | → | CI team blends these workforce generated opportunities into the project plan | → | Oppurtunities addressed quickly through *Kaizen* events | → | Results are visible to the workforce and influence the organization's culture |

Figure 9-1.

More and more Six Sigma practitioners have come to realize that by addressing the low-hanging fruit and identified waste within the project area, they can identify the causes of defects and variation faster and eliminate them. In connection with this, Six

Sigma Belts have come to value workforce involvement in waste elimination. A growing number of black belts and green belts now recognize the value of employees who are open to change and willing to participate in positive process change efforts.

This change in process improvement management has created an environment where change is accepted because employees are an integral part of the improvement cycle. Employees not only understand the need to change but they welcome it. They also assist project teams in implementing change, and this involvement creates ownership in the new process (see Fig. 9-2). Moreover, the speed at which change occurs in this environment defeats the old attitudes and concerns associated with "flavor of the month" change initiatives.

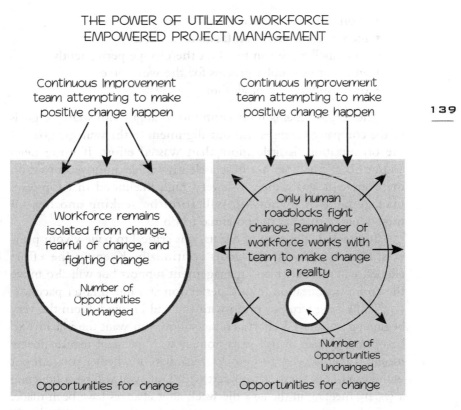

THE POWER OF UTILIZING WORKFORCE
EMPOWERED PROJECT MANAGEMENT

Continuous Improvement team attempting to make positive change happen

Continuous Improvement team attempting to make positive change happen

Workforce remains isolated from change, fearful of change, and fighting change

Number of Opportunities Unchanged

Opportunities for change

Only human roadblocks fight change. Remainder of workforce works with team to make change a reality

Number of Opportunities Unchanged

Opportunities for change

Figure 9-2.

Lay the Foundation for Sustaining the Gains

For any continuous improvement effort to be sustained over an extended period of time, the evolution in employee attitude described above is essential. If an organization's long-term CI vision and goals are to be realized, employees must believe that they have ownership in the process; they must also want the process and the organization to succeed.

Laying this foundation for sustaining process and financial gains (see Fig. 9-3) is a prerequisite to creating positive results that meet or exceed the expectations of management, stakeholders, the workforce and, ultimately, the customer. The results must be powerful enough to overcome any existing cultural barriers to change, and this means that they must demonstrate

- strong financial returns;
- increased customer satisfaction;
- a compelling reason to adopt the change permanently;
- an easier or simpler process for the workforce;
- or a combination of all four.

The improvements must continue to align with strategic goals of the company. Change, without alignment to the strategic goals of the organization, is little more than wasted effort. If using Lean and/or Six Sigma does not have a clearly visible, positive impact on these strategic goals, there is a very high likelihood that top-level management or ownership will soon be seeking another CI methodology that has the potential to do so.

To preclude this turn of events, it is critical to review your projects, results, and strategic goals continually. Keeping the effort aligned will not only retain management support but will also move the entire organization toward perfection at a much faster pace.

Think long term, or begin with the end in mind. From the very beginning of your CI efforts, consider how you want the initiative to be operating three to five years from now. Implement regular review meetings after the very first project, regardless of whether you start out with Lean or Six Sigma. If you start with Lean, you will be conducting a review meeting in the area the week after changes have been made.

If the goal is to adopt continuous improvement, you must begin to instill an absolute commitment to this goal immediately. There is no room for skepticism among the workforce that the initiative is another "flavor of the month"—your success in combating this skepticism depends on consistency and on communication that reinforces the importance of the initiative. This means enabling a cultural change, and the best way to succeed with this cultural change is to start it very early in the process.

Foundational Requirements to Sustain Gains

- Results must be powerful enough to overcome cultural barriers
  - Strong financial gains
  - Compelling reason to change
  - Easier, simpler process for employees
  - Or, a combination of the above
- Results must align with strategic goals
- Long-term thinking
- Conduct regular reviews
- Executive council, belts, managers and facilitators must follow through
- Communicate current conditions and results
  - Both good and bad

141

Figure 9-3.

Review meetings keep the initiative moving forward at a rapid pace. These meetings do not, and should not, take a considerable amount of time. Weekly review meetings within departments, groups, or areas should typically last no more than fifteen minutes. Starting with a discussion of what has happened within the past week can break the ice enough for most employees to open up and talk about successes and failures. The purpose of these meetings is to discuss issues that the workforce has run into during the week or those that persist over an extended period of time. Providing display boards in each area for the employees to write down these problems as they occur can jumpstart this discussion. Moving quickly from issues and opportunities to new ideas and/or solutions is the key to keeping the meetings short. You cannot allow the review meeting to evolve into complaint sessions. Close out each meeting by having the meeting facilitator discuss which problems and solutions/ideas can be addressed through Lean and which can be handled as a Six Sigma project.

The review meetings are valuable to the extent that the executive council and your belts, managers, and facilitators follow through. Ideas must be acted upon in a reasonable amount of time. Lean items should be addressed as soon as possible. Potential Six Sigma projects must be added to the list for the executive council to review. If the project is viable, a time frame must be established and communicated to the workforce. If a project is not viable, an explanation must be offered at the next review meeting explaining why it has been rejected.

Lean practitioners occasionally use these review meetings for point *kaizen*—i.e., an instantaneous *kaizen* event, which is quite similar to the Japanese concept of *kaizen*. Such events may last only 15 to 30 minutes and focus on recommendations to try something new or different, with input from everyone on the team. If the idea is feasible, it can be turned over to the employees for completion. However, until your continuous improvement culture is fully in place, this type of Lean improvement work should be the exception rather than the norm. Because human roadblocks have a tendency to drag out review meetings, as well as everything else, to avoid work, you are better served by using it as an occasional tool for true quick-hitting ideas rather than as a standard.

In conjunction with review meetings, display boards can be used to emphasize the concept of continuous improvement. These boards, as noted above, can be collection points for problems and opportunities as well as ideas. They should be updated regularly (daily or weekly), and the workforce should be made aware of changes during daily team meetings and/or as a part of the regular reviews. In addition to providing a collection points for problems and solutions, good display boards include some or all of the following:

- Value stream maps (current and future state)
- List of projects identified for the area and status of each
- Spaghetti diagrams of the area showing the travel path of people, products, and/or paper
- Before-and-after photos:
    - Baseline set before any changes were implemented
    - Before the most recent changes were implemented
    - After the most recent changes were implemented
- Quality metrics

- 5S audit reports
- Takt time
- Performance against takt time; or hour-by-the-day reports (which achieve the same thing on an ongoing hourly basis)
- Before-and-after metrics from previous project(s)

Create a Structure That Supports Continuous Improvement

To create a successful structure in which continuous improvement can live and flourish, an organization must do two things: *publicly recognize achievements and success* and keep moving forward. Each of these conditions for success is addressed below.

Recognize Achievements Publicly and Celebrate Successes

It is important that your employees see positive change and understand why this matters (see Fig. 9-4). They need to know how this change affects the bottom line of the organization and how it affects them *personally*. You can begin communicating this information on the display boards described earlier in this chapter. But to drive this message home, the best vehicle is celebration. Such celebrations have a dual purpose. While they recognize all employees for their efforts, they also underscore an organization's commitment to change and management's support of that commitment.

143

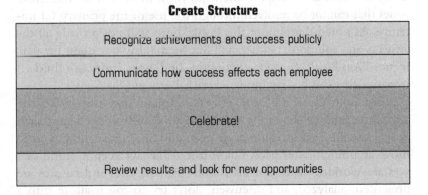

Create Structure

| Recognize achievements and success publicly |
| Communicate how success affects each employee |
| Celebrate! |
| Review results and look for new opportunities |

Figure 9-4.

Celebrations can range from simple memos circulated by email or placed in employee mailboxes to extravagant parties for the entire organization. You do not have to have a big blowout dinner or party every time a project is a success. You do, however, need to recognize success each and every time it occurs. Simple review meetings, attended by top-level managers who congratulate team members and workers, go a long way in achieving this recognition. Certificates of accomplishment, T-shirts, or even soda parties at break time can also create an atmosphere of celebration.

Keep Moving Forward

Although each success is cause to celebrate, you must never lose sight of the future. Keeping the future in view means emphasizing the need to keep moving toward perfection. Make sure your workforce understands that survival and growth means extending the organization's market share while continuously striving to reduce costs and improve quality. Without this reinforcement, the workforce may become complacent or even forget the reason for change. This erodes the culture of change and, once this occurs, processes may revert to "the old way" of doing things.

There are several things management can do to prevent this backward slide. Management should acknowledge and actively promote the existence of multiple CI initiatives and work to ensure that these multiple efforts are integrated into an almost seamless synchronized approach. Employees need to know that as an organization progresses along its continuous improvement journey, there will be numerous issues that cannot be resolved through the use of the primary CI initiative. As noted throughout this book, Lean will not provide all the answers and solutions; neither will Six Sigma. In your quest for perfection, you may even want to consider finding and adding a third CI initiative that can be synchronized with Lean and Six Sigma.

Embrace these multiple efforts, explain the strategy to the workforce, and celebrate the success of this multipronged approach. A synchronized effort using both Lean and Six Sigma allows you to move at a much faster pace, but you must always keep in mind that you are working with two disciplines. As successes and failures are presented, analyzed, and discussed, don't try to roll it all up into a single program just because is easier to explain to employees or simplifies public relations with your customers and suppliers. Call it what it is—continuous improvement—and don't be afraid to explain how it works. When Lean projects use Six-Sigma tools, include this information in reports, presentations, and team meetings. Likewise, when Six Sigma uses a Lean concept to remove low-hanging fruit or to implement change, let all employees see and understand what happened.

By creating an atmosphere of teamwork among initiatives (see Fig. 9-5), you show the workforce that the goal is continuous improvement, period. Any CI tool, concept, or idea that can be incorporated into the synchronized initiative, should be incorporated. Embrace it and use it to its maximum potential. This is not to say that you should constantly change directions, tools, and/or CI initiatives. Instead, you should find a way to wrap these additional efforts around the core efforts of Lean and Six Sigma, using them as add-on tools to enhance existing projects.

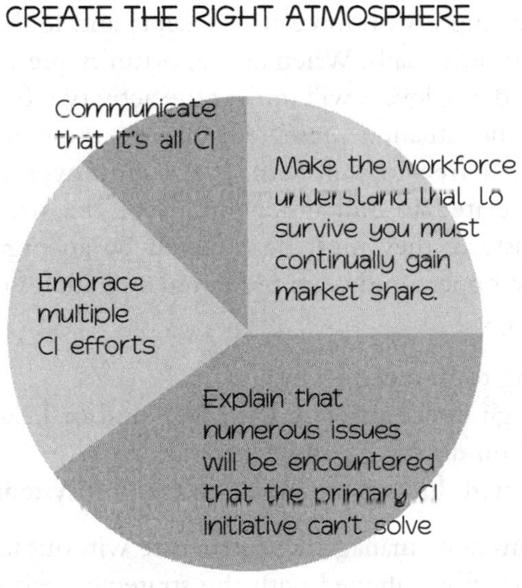

CREATE THE RIGHT ATMOSPHERE

Communicate that it's all CI

Make the workforce understand that to survive you must continually gain market share.

Embrace multiple CI efforts

Explain that numerous issues will be encountered that the primary CI initiative can't solve

Figure 9-5.

As your journey toward perfection progresses, your organization should begin to entrust more and more of the CI efforts to the process owners. Taking a page right out of Lean, the long-term success of the journey relies on an organization's ability to create common understanding of the reason for change. Managers, supervisors, and employees who understand why change is important are more likely to continue the effort on their own. These process owners should be encouraged to run their own review meetings as they learn the techniques and effectively identify problems and opportunities. The longer the CI effort exists, the more process owners must be involved in the change effort. The best strategy for the future is to integrate these process owners into more and more projects. The best people to work on these projects will be the CI managers, belts, and facilitators who emerge during the process, learn from it, and continuously improve upon it.

Focus on the Future

To complete the cultural change that enables an environment in which continuous improvement can truly exist as a way of life, an organization must focus on the future (see Fig. 9-6). It must also focus on creating a workforce that accepts and looks for improvement opportunities daily. When an opportunity presents itself, these self-motivated employees will initiate the activity required to correct or improve the situation presented. Clearly, these activities should not become a free-for-all with every employee implementing changes unrelated to and independent of the organization's CI structure. Instead, they must be directed by an organizational CI vision where opportunities are presented and addressed in *all* of the following ways:

- During team meetings
- Through direct dialogue with belts and/or Lean masters
- Listed on display boards
- Submitted through employee suggestion systems

Using this same management structure without fail will keep all improvement efforts aligned with the strategic goals of the organization. It will also coordinate CI efforts throughout the organization. Without this structure and coordination, you risk changes that can adversely affect other efforts, whether these are underway or already completed.

If it is done properly, transferring ownership of a process to the process owners creates *accountability* and additionally reinforces the

FOCUS ON THE FUTURE

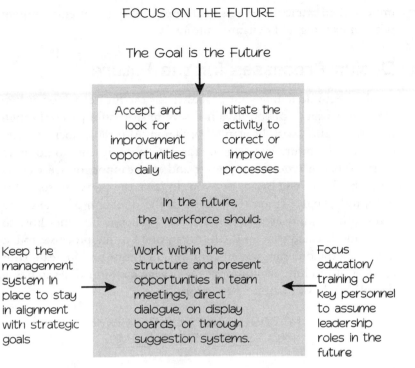

Figure 9-6.

culture of change. However, management must understand that accountability cannot be handed to the process owners who have no Lean or Six Sigma skill sets to rely on. Accountability must be transitioned over time as common understanding and skills are developed within the process.

Focusing on education and training of key personnel to assume leadership roles ensures the future stability of the synchronized initiative. Employees come and go. Key personnel, even in a very stable organization, do leave at some point, either to pursue an attractive professional opportunity or to retire. Successful, long-term sustainment relies on being prepared to deal with this contingency. By including employees identified as key people and process leaders, you are sustaining the momentum. You are also creating teams with leaders that have instant lines of communication as changes are made and/or identified. In some cases, you will be able to retain key personnel that other organizations fail to retain, because you have presented an attractive professional opportunity in an environment with an exciting and dynamic culture.

Design Processes for the Future

Finally, begin designing your processes for the future as soon as you can. Don't wait until you have had several successful passes through the organization with Lean and Six Sigma. Also remember that you can shape the future by preparing for it. Obviously, you do not have a crystal ball in your back pocket and you cannot foresee exactly what the future will bring. But you do have the power to see what exists today and a vision that points in the direction of where you want to be tomorrow and beyond. The challenge becomes how to accommodate and plan for the future in our existing processes today. That said, the one sure way to confront the future and increase your chances of reaching the tomorrow you have envisioned lies in being flexible while you aim for perfection.

THE BASIC TENETS OF DESIGNING
PROCESSES FOR THE FUTURE

148

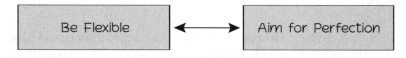

Figure 9-7.

Lean masters strive to build flexibility into process layout, cell design, and value streams. The thrust behind this is to expand or contract the value stream to accommodate more or less demand while eliminating waste. This is the vantage point from which all organizations should begin looking to the future. Create flexibility within the process while maintaining standardized work. Look at the strategic goals and find the vision of the future. As Lean and Six Sigma projects are implemented, keep this vision out in plain sight; use it as a guideline for process design. Be flexible. Be innovative. But most importantly, be customer focused.

Conclusion

There is much at stake if you fail to plan for the future: *initiative . . . your organization's culture . . . and your organization's ability to survive.* To survive in today's global economy, every company must be able to satisfy its customers' demands and exceed their expectations. This requires delivering

- what the customer wants (listening to the customer, quality of service or product);
- when the customer wants it (on-time delivery);
- at a fair price (this does not mean cheap; it means with high quality and little or no non-value-added processing).

To be good enough tomorrow you need to have a system in place today that will continually seek perfection and grow your market share. By utilizing the powerful tools of both Lean and Six Sigma it is possible to create such a system. Using a synchronized approach allows you to respond to the voice of the customer and be today what the competition is trying to be tomorrow. Remember that the journey to the future is about survival of the fittest . . . being good enough today is not good enough for tomorrow.

149

Whether you choose to be a gazelle or a lion is of no consequence.
It is enough to know that with the rising of the sun, you must run.
And you must run faster than you did yesterday or you will die.
This is the race of life.

This is the race of every organization today!

INDEX

Accelerated project results, 97–98
Accountability, 76, 146, 147
Administrative/management
   processes, 21
Amarillo Gear Company, 78–79
American companies, 56
Analyze phase, 49, 64, 104
Approach decisions, 116–19
Argent Global Services, 98–102
Assembly line, 67
Assignable cause, 45, 47, 97
Average project time, 100

Baseline data, 115
Beam's Industries, Inc., 31–35
Before-and-after photos, 142
Belts, 45, 47, 60, 135. *See also* Black
   belt; Green belt; Master black
   belt
Black belt, 83–84
   champion and, 41–42, 60
   in chartering process, 43
   finding defect sources, 53–54
   skills/traits of, 121–22
   training of, 48–50
   See also Green belt
Blended approach. *See* Integrated
   initiative
Bottom-line results, 13, 61–63, 65, 92,
   99, 100, 106
Brainstorming, 27, 86
Breakthrough approach, 57
Breakthrough moment, 34
Business unit lead team, 41, 42
"Buy-in" of employees, 27

Cabinet manufacturer case study,
   85–87
Capacity, 12
Case study
   gear manufacturer, 78–79

Lean, seat belt manufacturer, 31–35
Lean, then Six Sigma, 102–7
Lean vs. Six Sigma, 66–69
   plastics manufacturer, 48–50
Six Sigma, cabinet manufacturer,
   85–87
Six Sigma, electrical circuits, 107–9
Six Sigma, paper manufacturing,
   63–66
Celebrating successes, 143–44
Champion, 40, 41–42, 60, 82–83
Change. *See* Culture of positive
   change
Charter, 42–44
CI. *See* Continuous improvement
Closure and review loop, 136
Combined approach. *See* Integrated
   initiative
Commitment to excellence, 4
Communication, 112–13
Competitive advantage
   at Beam's Industries, Inc., 34
   continuous improvement and, 3–6
   dramatic improvements and, 66
Computer software, 132
Consolidated management, 8
Consultants, 34
Continuous improvement (CI)
   accomplishments using, 2
   blended approach, 89–90
   continual reminders for, 10–11
   incremental improvement and, 5
   Lean, 26–27, 30, 55, 74
   multiple initiatives, 144–46
   real use of, 4
   stage, Lean, 30
   structure, creation of, 143–46
   team, 139
   as ultimate goal, 3
   See also Lean; Process improvement;
      Six Sigma

151

ABOUT THE AUTHORS

Mark Nash is a managing director for Argent Global Services. He has 23 years of process improvement experience, both as an internal and external consultant/engineer, in manufacturing, distribution, and health care. He spent ten years working for the State of Oklahoma, including time as a legislative auditor, a fiscal analyst for the Oklahoma State Senate, and as director of finance for the Department of Public Safety. He has considerable experience with financial and management analysis. This diversified background allows Mark to work outside the box looking for process solutions many people cannot visualize.

Since joining Argent in 1994, Mark has completed transactional reviews and process improvement projects for numerous organizations worldwide. These projects and reviews focused on purchasing, central support staff, transportation, order entry, supply chain management, and product engineering, as well as transformations and Six Sigma project management. Mark's experience in Lean Healthcare includes assisting organizations in both the United States and the United Kingdom with Lean transformations. Additionally Mark and his Lean team at Argent Global Services have developed a unique introductory Lean training seminar that includes a four-round laboratory simulation.

A multiskilled Six Sigma black belt, Mark is also a certified NIST/MEP trainer, currently partnering with the Oklahoma Alliance for Manufacturing Excellence to provide Lean manufacturing training throughout the State of Oklahoma. Over the past five years, Mark has facilitated more than 350 Lean classes and workshops dealing with principles of Lean manufacturing, value stream mapping, the 5S system, pull/*kanban* systems, setup reduction, and total productive maintenance (TPM).

Sheila R. Poling is a managing partner of Pinnacle Partners, Inc. With more than twenty years' experience in the quality and productivity industry, she previously served as vice president of two nationally recognized consulting/training firms and a book publishing firm. Her management responsibilities have included managing twenty-five consultants and administrative staff. Sheila's broad professional experience includes work in operations management, product, training materials and seminar development, marketing and sales, client interface, and customer satisfaction initiatives focused on business excellence with an emphasis on leadership and quality.

A prolific writer, Sheila has coauthored several books, including the internationally recognized *Customer Focused Quality*, a book on customer satisfaction and service; and *Building Continual Improvement: SPC for the Service Industry and Administrative Areas.* She has served as a primary editor for a featured monthly column in *Quality Magazine* and is coauthor of *Brain Teasers: Real-world Challenges to Build Your Manufacturing Skills*, published by *Quality*. McGraw-Hill's *The Manufacturing Engineering Handbook*, released in 2004, features her chapter on "Six Sigma and Lean Implementation."

Sheila has also coauthored several work manuals, including "Perfecting Continual Improvement Skills" and "Strategy-Driven Six Sigma: A Champion Overview." In addition, she has helped design multiple course offerings focused on leadership training, organizational and operations excellence, Six Sigma, and statistical process control. She is currently serving on the American Society for Quality's Six Sigma committee and on the Innovation Research committee.

Sheila holds a degree in Business Administration from the University of Tennessee and is a senior member of the American Society for Quality as well as a member of the American Marketing and Management Associations and ISSSP. She has also had the privilege to study and work closely with many distinguished industry leaders, including Dr. W. Edwards Deming.

Dr. Sophronia "Frony" Ward is a managing partner of Pinnacle Partners, Inc. She is a statistician and continual improvement expert who specializes in Six Sigma, Lean Six Sigma, and Statistical Process Control training, consulting, and coaching. Specializing in black belt, green belt, and master black belt training and certification, Frony is currently sharing her expertise with numerous companies in her capacity as senior master black belt.

Since 1981, Frony has served as consultant to numerous automotive, government, glass, chemical, paint, health-care, telecommunications, and food companies, assisting in the implementation of quality management and tools for continual improvement. She has been a lead consultant and/or trainer with Harley Davidson, IBM Corporation, Northrup-Grumann, NASA, Dow Chemical, Scripps Health, Social Security Administration, Novant Healthcare, Metzeler Automotive Profile Systems, IRS, Republic Paper, MacSteel, BellSouth and other organizations.

While a professor at the University of Tennessee, Frony was one of four founders of the university's internationally recognized Institute for Productivity through Quality. Since that time, she has earned a well-deserved reputation for her work within and beyond U.S. borders. Her wide-ranging international experience includes teaching and consulting in Venezuela, Canada, Mexico, Chile, Thailand, France, Australia, and South Africa. In 1984, she joined a major consulting firm as a senior consultant and director of consulting services. While serving in this capacity, she designed a highly successful three-week seminar that was held in the United States, Mexico, and Venezuela. She also helped to design a successful Design of Experiments seminar. Today, she provides training and coaching for Six Sigma in more than thirty different companies in five countries. Dr. Sophronia Ward has developed the popular workshop and workbook, *SPC: Getting Started*, and codeveloped the curriculum and course materials for the seminar, *Perfecting Continual Improvement Skills*. She is also the designer of the popular SPC software package, **improvIT**. For the past four years she has been the featured monthly columnist for *Quality Magazine*'s "Brain Teasers," a column recently hailed as the magazine's most widely read feature. This monthly column lead *Quality* magazine to publish her book, *Brain Teasers: Real-world Challenges to Build Your Manufacturing Skills*. In addition, McGraw-Hill's *The Manufacturing Engineering Handbook*, released in 2004, features her chapter on "Six Sigma and Lean Implementation."

Dr. Sophronia Ward received her B.S. in statistics from North Carolina State University and her Ph.D. in statistics from Virginia Tech. She is a senior member of the American Society of Quality and is a member of the American Statistical Association. She also holds certification in Myers-Brigg Type Indicator and SMYLOG (a team dynamics survey instrument).